KEYNOTE

Music to GCSE

TIM CAIN

CAMBRIDGE UNIVERSITY PRESS

Cambridge

New York   New Rochelle   Melbourne   Sydney

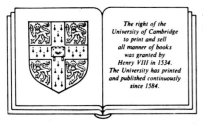

The right of the University of Cambridge to print and sell all manner of books was granted by Henry VIII in 1534. The University has printed and published continuously since 1584.

Published by the Press Syndicate of the University of Cambridge
The Pitt Building, Trumpington Street, Cambridge CB2 1RP
32 East 57th Street, New York, NY 10022, USA
10 Stamford Road, Oakleigh, Melbourne 3166, Australia

© Cambridge University Press 1988

First published 1988

Printed in Great Britain by Scotprint Ltd, Musselburgh, Scotland

ISBN 0 521 33821 2

Author's acknowledgements

Grateful thanks to Nick Barlow who devised the theme and most of the lesson plan for chapter 10, Angela Havens who supervised the typing, and to the following who provided criticism, advice and inspiration: Robert Bunting, Annie Cave, Rosemary Davidson, Reg Fletcher, Fiona Harvey, Mary King, Robert Kwami, Cliff Matthews, George Odam, Amanda Ogden, Frances Sheppherd and Keith Swanwick and Geoffrey White.

Thanks also to my wife Ann, without whom none of it would have been possible. It is to her that this book is, with love, dedicated.

Publisher's acknowledgements

Thanks are due to the following for permission to use extracts from material in their copyright:

p.15 'Love Me Tender', words and music by Elvis Presley © 1956 Elvis Presley Music Co., USA, reproduced by permission of Carlin Music Ltd & International Music Publications; pp.23, 24 'Matwala Jiya' from *Mother India*, The Gramophone Company of India Ltd; p.35 'E Saiye Re' and p.36 'Maajo' from *Synchro Sound* performed by King Sunny Adé, © 1983 Island Music Ltd, ALL RIGHTS RESERVED used by permission; pp.39, 41 *Carmina Burana* by Carl Orff, Schott & Co. Ltd; p.51 'Bye Bye Love' by Felice and Boudleaux Bryant, recorded by Simon and Garfunkel on *Bridge Over Troubled Water* © 1957 House of Bryant Publishing, USA, Acuff Rose Music Inc., London W1, reproduced with the permission of Music Sales Ltd, London W1; p.53 'The Boxer' by Paul Simon, Pattern Music Ltd; p.77 'The Wife of the Soldier' by Bertolt Brecht, as used in translation in *Byker Hill*, performed by Martin Carthy, credit to David Swarbrick and Martin Carthy, and p.79 'Lucy Wan' from *Byker Hill*, performed by Martin Carthy, both reproduced by permission of The Sparta Florida Music Group Ltd, London; pp.82 'Crazy Baldheads' and pp.83–4 'War', performed by Bob Marley and the Wailers © 1976 Bob Marley Music Ltd BV, reproduced by permission of Rondor Music (London) Ltd; pp.94–5 'Ionisation' by Varèse © Colfranc Music Corpn NY, Agent: E C Kerby Ltd, Toronto, Ricordi-Chesham, reprinted by arrangement; p.109 'West End Blues', words and music by Joseph Oliver and Clarence Williams © 1928 Clarence Williams Publishing Co., USA, sub-published B Feldman & Co. Ltd, London WC2H 0LD, reproduced by permission of EMI Music Publishing Ltd & International Music Publications.

Photocopying of pages containing the copyright material listed here is illegal. They are specifically excluded from any blanket photocopying arrangements.

Artwork by Geraldine Marchand. Cover design by Geraldine Marchand.

TO THE TEACHER

Please feel free to adapt the materials in this book in any way
you wish to suit the best interests of yourself and your
students. With regard to the 'Quiz' sections, these have been
designed for teaching as much as for testing. Ideally, every
student would be able to play back sections of the music as
often as is necessary to answer the questions at his or her own
pace. Although this is not often possible, the overriding
principle is that the students should get to know the music of
the Quizzes well enough to be able to enjoy it.

COMPONENTS OF THE KEYNOTE COURSE

Course Book   ISBN 0 521 33821 2

Set of 2 Cassettes   ISBN 0 521 35457 9

Teacher's Handbook   ISBN 0 521 33822 0

CONTENTS

Handwritten annotations: CASSETTE 1 SIDE A; 1A; 1A; 2A (start); 1A; (No); 1A; 2A; 1B (start); (No); 2A School; 2A (middle and end); 2B (start); 1B; 1B; 2B School; 2B

CONTENTS *contd*

RECORD LIST

Medieval
Dances from the Danserye by Susato   Two Renaissance Dance Bands   HQS 1249

Rock & Roll
20 Greatest Hits Vol. One by Elvis Presley   *½*   CBS NL 89024

Symphony No. 5 by Beethoven (First Movement)   *RECORD*   Several recordings available

Indian
Mother India
performed by Lata Mangeshkar   Gramophone Company of India   3AEX 5001*

Beat Sgt. Pepper's Lonely Hearts Club Band by The Beatles   EMI 14C 064 04177

African Synchro System by King Sunny Adé and his African Beats   Island ILPS 9737

Carmina Burana by Carl Orff   Several recordings available

Impressionistic
Syrinx by Debussy   Several recordings available

Bridge Over Troubled Water by Simon and Garfunkel   CBS 63699

The Young Person's Guide to the Orchestra by Benjamin Britten   Several recordings available

RECORD
Symphony No. 9 'From the New World' by Dvořák   Several recordings available

Symphony No. 94 in G 'The Surprise' by Haydn   Several recordings available

Folk Byker Hill performed by Martin Carthy   Topic 12TS 342*

Reggae Rastaman Vibration by Bob Marley and the Wailers   Island ILPS 19498

Clarinet Trio by Mozart (Second Movement)   Several recording available

Contemp *RECORD*
Ionisation by Varèse   Several recordings available

'Danse Macabre' by Saint-Saëns   *RECORD*   Several recordings available

Jazz 'West End Blues' performed by Louis Armstrong and his Hot Five
Louis Armstrong: Greatest Hits   BBC REB 597

Violin Concerto in E by Bach   *RECORD*   Several recordings available

Dichterliebe by Schumann   *RECORD*   Several recordings available

* see Teacher's Book for list of suppliers

MUSIC TIME CHART

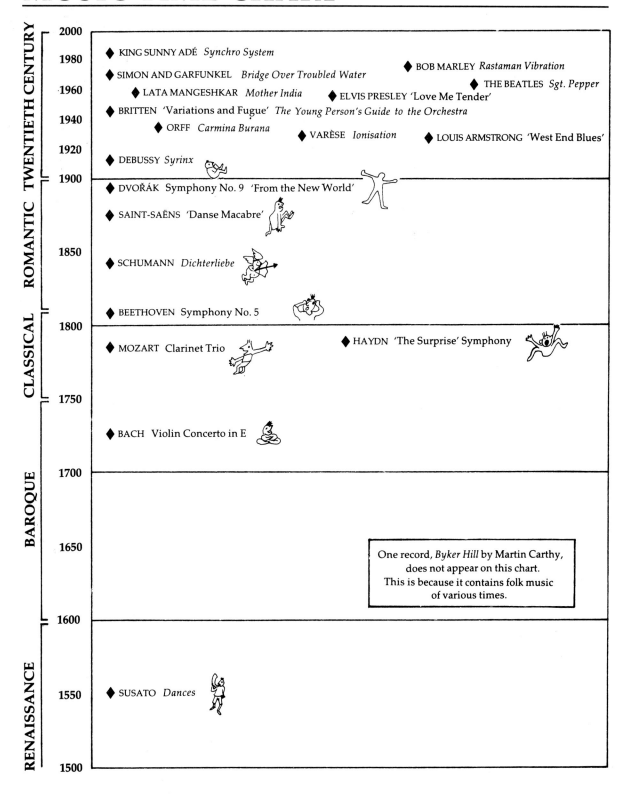

TWENTIETH CENTURY

2000

1980 — ◆ KING SUNNY ADÉ *Synchro System*

◆ BOB MARLEY *Rastaman Vibration*

◆ SIMON AND GARFUNKEL *Bridge Over Troubled Water*

1960 — ◆ THE BEATLES *Sgt. Pepper*

◆ LATA MANGESHKAR *Mother India* ◆ ELVIS PRESLEY 'Love Me Tender'

◆ BRITTEN 'Variations and Fugue' *The Young Person's Guide to the Orchestra*

1940

◆ ORFF *Carmina Burana* ◆ VARÈSE *Ionisation* ◆ LOUIS ARMSTRONG 'West End Blues'

1920

◆ DEBUSSY *Syrinx*

1900

ROMANTIC

◆ DVOŘÁK Symphony No. 9 'From the New World'

◆ SAINT-SAËNS 'Danse Macabre'

1850

◆ SCHUMANN *Dichterliebe*

◆ BEETHOVEN Symphony No. 5

1800

CLASSICAL

◆ MOZART Clarinet Trio ◆ HAYDN 'The Surprise' Symphony

1750

◆ BACH Violin Concerto in E

1700

BAROQUE

1650

> One record, *Byker Hill* by Martin Carthy,
> does not appear on this chart.
> This is because it contains folk music
> of various times.

1600

RENAISSANCE

1550 — ◆ SUSATO *Dances*

1500

1 WORKING WITH RHYTHMS

DANCES FROM THE DANSERYE by Susato

Susato was famous mainly as a publisher. He lived and worked in Antwerp in Belgium during the first half of the sixteenth century (during what is called the **Renaissance***) composing, **arranging** and publishing music. The dances in his book *The Danserye* were arranged by him from the popular songs and instrumental music that were probably the sixteenth century's equivalent of our *Smash Hits*. He also published many volumes of serious music, including a lot of religious music.

* Words in bold type are explained at the back of the book.

START

Tap or clap these rhythmic *figures:*

Join some of these **rhythms** together to make a long rhythmic **phrase**. Practise it several times until you can play it smoothly without gaps or hesitations.

Tap or clap your rhythmic phrase to the rest of your class. As you listen to the others, try to tell which rhythmic figures they use, and in which order.

LISTEN

Listen to 'Pavane La Bataille' (see **pavane**) by Susato. Which rhythmic figure is repeated many times?
Which rhythmic figure is played a few times just before the end?

Listen again, and quietly tap these rhythms in time with the drummer on the recording. When does the drummer play more softly?

COMPOSE

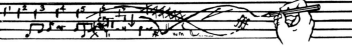

Compose a piece using rhythmic figures. You will need an **untuned percussion** instrument.

○ FIRST experiment to find as many different **tone colours** as you can from your instrument — but treat it with care!

○ NEXT, using these tone colours, make the following:
Some rhythmic figures which are very fast.
Some rhythmic figures which are very soft.
Some rhythmic figures which use two or more tone colours.
Some rhythmic figures which feel hesitant.
Some rhythmic figures which feel quietly confident.

○ FINALLY choose some of these rhythmic figures and put them together to make a piece which contains a surprise somewhere in it.

PERFORM

Perform your music to the rest of your class. As you listen to the others, decide whether each piece varies the *dynamics* effectively.

'La Mourisque' by Susato

FIRST PLAYING

1 Which of these words most nearly describes the character of this music?

a. relaxed   b. majestic   c. aggressive

2 Is the *tempo* of the music fast, medium or slow?

SECOND PLAYING

3 This music is in three sections:

    A the first section
    B a contrasting section, slightly quieter
    A the first section repeated

Raise your hand when you hear the beginning of section B, and again when you hear section A for the second time.

THIRD PLAYING

4   Play these rhythmic figures. Which of them is played many times by the drummer?

5   How many times does the drummer play this rhythm?

6   With what does the music begin and end?

RESEARCH

1   Find out what 'Renaissance' means, and when the 'Renaissance period' was. Prepare a report for the rest of your class on:

   one Renaissance composer (e.g. Byrd, Lassus, Victoria, Palestrina)

   or one Renaissance artist (e.g. Michelangelo, Leonardo, Raphael)

   Find out when and where your musician or artist lived, and describe at least one example of his work.

2   Find out about these Renaissance instruments: cornett, sackbut, crumhorn, lute and viol. For each one, discover what it looks like, how it is played, and what it sounds like.

3   In Renaissance times, songs were often performed as instrumental pieces. Find a modern piece that has been recorded both as a song and as an instrumental piece. Listen to both, and decide what the main differences are.

Dances from *Terpsichore* by Praetorius

RENAISSANCE INSTRUMENTS

Although these were written over fifty years later, they have a lot in common with Susato's collection. The lively dances have a bounding, brash energy, and there are some beautiful slow dances too. There is a particularly effective recording by David Munrow and the Early Music Consort of London, the same performers as on your recording of Susato's dances.

Mass for Five Voices by Byrd

CHOIR

This **mass** was written near the end of the Renaissance period, and is among the greatest pieces of music ever written for the Christian church. The best way of getting to know this profound and subtle music is by singing it, but it is possible to appreciate it by attentive listening. Start by getting to know the last **movement**, the 'Agnus Dei'. If you can find a musical **score**, you might enjoy singing along with the recording.

2 MAKING A MELODY

you ain't nuthin' but a houn' dog

20 GREATEST HITS VOL. ONE
Elvis Presley

Rock'n'roll is for many people the most exciting **style** of pop music – the beginning of the '**rock** revolution'. Its main features are a driving rhythmic **beat** helped by a loud and assertive drum kit and, in later rock'n'roll, more and more electric instruments, particularly electric guitars.

Elvis was 'The King' with a string of hits during his short life. His voice was amazing: it was very powerful and capable of sounding sweet-toned or rough, tender or aggressive, depending on the song. His stage act was sensational, and was said to be outrageously suggestive.

Although he is now dead, he lives on in the hearts and minds of many people and pop music would not have been the same without him.

COMPOSE

Make a melody. You can use any melodic instrument.

○ FIRST decide which **pitches** to use. You will probably find it helpful to choose only six or seven different pitches, e.g. G, C, D, E, F and G[1].

○ THEN make a rhythmic figure two or four bars long. Write it down and practise it many times to fix it in your mind.

○ NEXT send it over the pitches you have chosen in the following ways:
Make some phrases in which one pitch is repeated 5 or 6 times.
Make some phrases in which the pitches go up by step.
Make some phrases in which the pitches go up then down (or down then up).
Make some phrases in which there is a mixture of steps and leaps.

○ FINALLY put some of these ideas together, perhaps with other ideas of your own, to make a **melody** which contains some sort of musical climax.

PERFORM
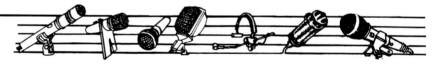

Perform your melody to the rest of the class.

As you listen to the others, decide whether each one sounds 'finished' or not. Is there a right note for ending on if you want the effect of sounding 'finished'?

LISTEN

You have probably noticed that the most memorable melodies are not necessarily the most complicated. Listen to 'Love Me Tender', a simple but expressive melody, performed by Elvis Presley. As you listen you can follow the melody, and later you can perform it yourself, perhaps in a different way from Elvis.

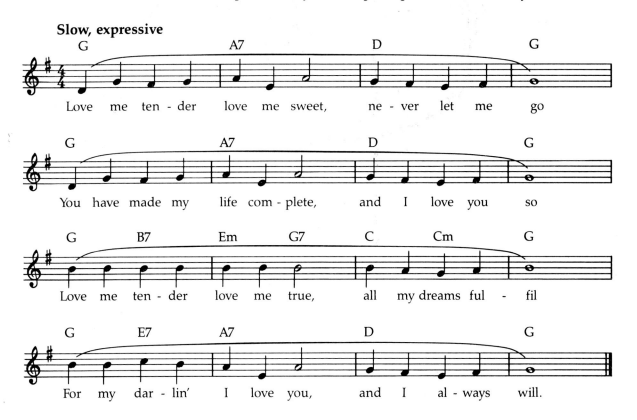

Slow, expressive

Love me ten - der love me sweet, ne - ver let me go

You have made my life com - plete, and I love you so

Love me ten - der love me true, all my dreams ful - fil

For my dar - lin' I love you, and I al - ways will.

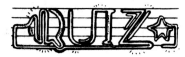

'Love Me Tender' by Elvis Presley

FIRST PLAYING

1 Which of these words would best describe the *tempo* of this song?
   a. grave   b. moderato   c. allegro   d. presto

2 What instruments are used in this song?

3 Apart from Elvis, what singers do you hear?

SECOND PLAYING

4 Which of these words would best describe the *dynamics* of this song?
   a. piano   b. mezzo forte   c. forte   d. fortissimo

5 What differences are there between the verses?

'Heartbreak Hotel' by Elvis Presley

FIRST PLAYING

1 How many verses are there in this song?

2 How many bars are there in each verse?

SECOND PLAYING

3 In the first two phrases, how many different notes does Elvis sing?

4 In which verse does the piano first play as a solo instrument?

5 Which two instruments play solos in the instrumental **break**?

6 Which of these two songs do you think is more effective, and why?

RESEARCH

1 Find out about the following styles: rhythm'n'blues, country music, punk.
Name   a. the main features   b. the main artists.
Describe one song in each style.

2 Find out more about Elvis. In particular, try to discover the differences between the songs he sang when he first started (e.g. 'Old Shep'), those which he sang in rock'n'roll style (e.g. 'Jailhouse Rock'), and his ballad-style songs (e.g. 'Are You Lonesome Tonight?').

3 Find out about one singer (or group) who has been in the charts recently, and who sings rock'n'roll. Listen to one of the songs, and compare it with any rock'n'roll song by Elvis. What are the main differences between them?

TRY THIS

'Rock Around the Clock' by Bill Haley and the Comets

'Rock Around the Clock' caused a sensation when it appeared in a film of the same name, and it has the reputation of being the first song ever in rock'n'roll style. It has a strong beat, but there is an easy, relaxed feel to it. The melody is simple but very memorable.

Music by Chuck Berry

Rock'n'roll has its roots in the music of the American blacks, so it is not surprising that one of its most popular singers was a black musician, Chuck Berry. He was a fine guitarist and had an unusual vocal style. Listen to one of his rock'n'roll classics such as 'Roll Over Beethoven', or 'Johnny B Goode'.

3 USING REPEATS

SYMPHONY NO. 5
by Beethoven
(First Movement)

Ludwig van Beethoven is thought to be one of the greatest of
all European composers. In musical terms he was a
revolutionary composer. At first he wrote music in the *classical*
style, like Haydn and Mozart. Then using unusual *keys* and
harmonies, longer and more complex forms, and a greater
range of orchestral and pianistic *timbres*, he made a
new style of music. This was less refined than the classical
style, but more forceful and vigorous. Many later composers
were influenced by Beethoven's music.

START

How can you make a reasonably long piece of music out of just one or two ideas?

One way is by using repeats. Any musical idea can be repeated either exactly or with small changes. Even a single sound can be repeated with small changes in tone colour, pitch, dynamics or length.

Try this yourself. Make any sound and repeat it many times, changing it slightly each time. How many changes can you make without the sound becoming completely different?

COMPOSE

Construct a melody by using repeats. You will need a melodic instrument.

○ FIRST make a short phrase. This will be the basis of your whole melody, so spend some time getting it right. Start by making a short, interesting rhythmic figure, then send it over three or four notes. Practise it and write it down.

○ NEXT try the following:
Repeat the phrase with each note up (or down) a step.
Repeat the phrase suddenly much louder (or softer).
Repeat the phrase so that it sounds more mysterious, then more angry.
Repeat the phrase with an added note or two.
Repeat the phrase using a different tone colour.
Repeat the phrase up (or down) an *octave*.

○ FINALLY put some of these ideas together to make a piece of music which contains some changes of mood, and also some rests.

PERFORM

Perform your melody with repeats.

When you listen to the others in your class, think about these questions:

Are some repeats more effective than others?
Can you have too many repeats?

LISTEN

Listen to the first movement of Beethoven's Fifth **Symphony**. What sort of repeats are there in this music?

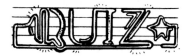

Symphony No. 5, First Movement (exposition section)

FIRST PLAYING

1 Which of these words best describes the character of this music?
a. relaxed   b. dreamy   c. delicate   d. forceful

2 Does the music start *p, mf* or *ff*?

3 Is it played by a **string** quartet, an orchestra or a **brass band**?

SECOND PLAYING

4 Does the music start in **unison** or in harmony?

5 Listen for this music:

Is it played by horns, clarinets or violins?

THIRD PLAYING

6 Raise your hand whenever you hear a rest in the music.

FOURTH PLAYING

7 Name some of the ways in which the music uses contrasts.

8 Does the music end *p, mf* or *ff*?

RESEARCH

1   Find out what a classical symphony is, and explain
    a. how many movements a symphony usually has, and
    b. which of these movements are usually fast, and which ones
       are slow.
    When you have done this, listen carefully to any *one* movement
    of a symphony by Haydn, Mozart, Beethoven or Schubert and
    describe it in detail.

2   Describe the instruments that normally play in a symphony,
    and explain how each one is played and how they are divided
    into sections.

3   Listen to the whole of the first movement of Beethoven's Fifth
    Symphony. Then write a description of this movement as if
    you were writing a programme-note for a concert. Describe the
    music in a way that will make people want to listen to it!

TRY THIS

Symphony No. 7 by Beethoven

ORCHESTRA

Beethoven wrote nine symphonies, and each one is
wonderfully expressive: in one moment there may be empty
despair, in the next overpowering joy. The Seventh Symphony
is a good example, particularly the second movement which
starts with a hushed and solemn death march, rises to a
passionate climax, and has a moment of tranquillity before the
ominous sound of the death march returns.

'Moonlight' Sonata by Beethoven

PIANO

The first movement of this *sonata* is particularly beautiful –
peaceful and placid. There are several arrangements that you
can buy and play – not quite the real thing, but fairly easy if
you are about grade 3/4 standard. You might attempt the real
thing if your playing is of around grade 6 standard.

4 USING A DRONE

मतवाला जिया

MOTHER INDIA performed by Lata Mangeshkar

India has one of the biggest film industries in the world, and its 'stars' are just as glamorous as those of the great Hollywood movies. Nearly all Indian films include music and dancing, and their stories are often very romantic. The music is sometimes just like American film music, but it is often based on Indian folk songs, and is sometimes a fusion of Western orchestral styles with Indian classical and folk styles.

In Indian films the actors and actresses do not normally sing, but their songs are 'dubbed' onto the sound-track by singers. The most popular of all these singers is Lata Mangeshkar. Her voice is considered so outstandingly beautiful that she has made nearly 2,000 films, and she has released more recordings than anyone else in the world.

LISTEN

Listen to 'Matwala Jiya' from *Mother India*. What sort of drums do you hear? What do you think they look like? What other **percussion** instrument do you hear?

Indian drums are called **tabla**. The larger drum (called 'biyah') can make several low pitches, and can even change pitch as it is hit. (Listen to this effect on the recording.) The higher drum (called 'tabla') has only one pitch, and must be tuned to the right pitch before it is played.

This effect – having one pitch played all through the music – is called a **drone**, and in 'Matwala Jiya' the drone is B♭. In a lot of Indian music there are two notes in the drone, e.g. B♭ and E♭. Listen again, to hear when the drone fits well with the rest of the music and when it makes a slightly disturbing, **discordant** effect.

Now play this drone together with some of the melody notes from 'Matwala Jiya'.

drone   melody notes

Which melody notes make a **concordant** (restful) effect with the drone? Which notes make a discordant (scrunchy) effect with the drone?

COMPOSE

Compose some music using a drone. You will need any melodic instrument that can play two notes at a time, and can also play the melody notes shown above.

○ FIRST play the drone. This can be a long, held note or it can have a rhythm. Use B♭ and E♭ as well if you like.

○ NEXT make the following:
Some phrases which start low and end up high.
Some phrases which are quick and light, and end on the same pitch as a drone.
Some phrases which hover around the pitch of the drone.
Some phrases which contain leaps.
Some phrases in which discordant sounds are followed by concordant ones.

○ FINALLY remember the best of the phrases that you discover – it will help to write them down. Then choose the phrases that sound best together to make your melody. Organise them whichever way you think is best, and do not be afraid of repeating phrases! Remember to keep this music – you will use it again in chapter 5.

PERFORM

Perform your music to the rest of your class. As you listen to the others, listen for the tension and relaxation that the discordant and concordant sounds make.

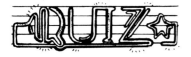

'Matwala Jiya'

This song contains several different melodies. The two most important ones begin like this:

MELODY A

MELODY B

Play them, and repeat them until you have the sound of each one firmly in your head.

FIRST PLAYING

1 When the orchestra begins, does it play melody A, melody B or a different melody?

2 When the singing begins, is it with melody A, melody B or a different melody?

3 During the first verse (until the orchestra plays on its own again) do you hear this melody once, twice or three times?

SECOND PLAYING

4 Arrange these in the order in which you hear them in the first verse:
   a. female *solo* (Lata Mangeshkar)
   b. female *chorus*
   c. male solo (Mohamad Rafi)
   d. male chorus

5 What is the difference between the singers in the second verse and those in the third?

THIRD PLAYING

6 How many times in the whole song do you hear melody A?

FOURTH PLAYING

7 How many times do you hear melody B?

8 How many times does the orchestra play on its own?

FIFTH PLAYING

9 In the last verse you hear Mohamad Rafi singing with the female chorus. Immediately after, you hear Lata Mangeshkar. Does she sing with   a. the female chorus   b. the male chorus   c. Mohamad Rafi?

SIXTH PLAYING

10 Name some of the ways in which the composer of this music has used repeats.

RESEARCH

1 Find out about the following Indian instruments: harmonium, tabla, sitar and tampura. What does each one look like, how is it played, and what does it sound like?

2 Find out everything you can about one aspect of India: its food, its art, its clothes, religions or history. Make a report for the rest of your class about the similarities and differences between this aspect of life in India and that of your own country.

3 Experiment with drones. Find two or three different melodies that you can play, and perform them using the keynote (*tonic*) as a drone. Which melodies work best? Can you think of any other type of music which uses drones?

TRY THIS

West Meets East by Ravi Shankar and Yehudi Menuhin

During the 1960s many Western musicians became interested in Indian classical music. Among them were George Harrison (one of the Beatles) and Yehudi Menuhin, a famous classical violinist. Menuhin loves Indian classical music, and when he had studied it for several years he felt able to perform it in public. This record is one result of his years of study, and he performs with an Indian friend of his, Ravi Shankar. The first side contains three short *ragas*, and the last one in particular is very attractive and exciting, especially when the music gets faster and faster towards the end.

Dance With Alaap by Alaap

This is dance music with a difference! The blend of styles on this recording is quite astonishing, as is the range of instruments used. Listening to Alaap, you will probably recognise the drones, the tabla rhythms and the curving, swooping melodies typical of a lot of Indian music. However, you will probably detect Greek, Spanish and accordian folk music influences all overlaid with a beat that is totally modern.

5 TERNARY FORM

The Beatles – John Lennon, Paul McCartney, George Harrison and Ringo Starr – have been called 'the most successful pop group of all time'. Between 1962, when they released their first single, and 1971, when they split up, they released a succession of hits such as no one before or after has ever equalled.

They sang about subjects that no rock singer had even considered such as the loneliness of a funeral service ('Eleanor Rigby') or suburban life ('Penny Lane'). They brought tone colours such as string **quartets**, brass bands and fairground organs into rock music, and they were among the first rock groups to use **electronic music** techniques. *Sgt. Pepper* is generally considered to be their best LP and is a good example of these aspects of their music.

START

Do you remember the work you did in chapter 1? If you do, you may remember that 'La Mourisque' had two different sections, A and B. The way that these are put together makes the **form** of the music. One of the simplest forms is A B A, called 'ternary form'. 'A Day in the Life' by The Beatles is in ternary form. See if you can hear this.

Ternary form A B A

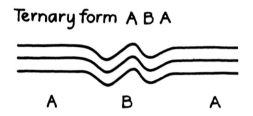

A   B   A

LISTEN

Listen to 'A Day in the Life'. Which words begin section A? Section B? Section A for the second time?

Listen again, and compare the two sections. Do it like this. Copy the following list. Next to each item write 'S' if they are the same (or fairly similar) in each section, and 'D' if they are completely different:

tone colours (instruments and voices)
words
melodies
tempo (speed)
dynamics (volume – loud/soft)

You probably found some things different, but other things fairly similar. This is because to be really effective, the middle (B) section must be *different* enough to make a good contrast, but *similar* enough to sound like the same piece of music.

COMPOSE

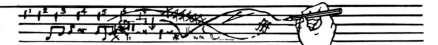

Compose a piece of music in ternary form. You will need the same instrument that you used in the last chapter.

○ FIRST start with the 'drone piece' that you made in chapter 4. Decide whether this is going to make the outer (A) sections or the middle (B) section. Also decide which elements are going to be the same, and which are going to be different in your new section. Choose from this list: drone, tone colours, dynamics, tempo, mood.

○ NEXT decide which notes you are going to use in your new section. Use five or six of the notes that you used in your 'drone music'. Choose from these notes:

But you may like to use one or two different notes. Choose from these:

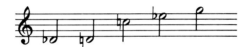

○ THEN remembering which elements will be the same, and which will be different, make your new section. If you like, you can follow the instructions that you followed in chapter 2 (p. 14) or chapter 3 (p. 19).

○ FINALLY put the piece together, listening carefully to the way in which the sections are joined. Do you want one section to flow into the next, or do you want a sudden shift in the music?

Here are some of the ways you could make the changes smooth:

> Use a **rallentando** at the end of your section A, and/or section B.
> Use the same note at the end of one section, and the beginning of the next.
> Repeat the last bar or two of one section to make a link with the next section.
> Use the same rhythmic patterns in both sections.

To help you decide, listen to the way the sections are joined in 'A Day in the Life'. When you have finished, write down the music.

PERFORM

Perform your music to the rest of your class. While you are listening to the others, try to decide what makes a good ternary form piece. Which pieces sound as if they have real unity?

'Getting Better' by The Beatles

FIRST VERSE

1   Which of these words best describes the opening of 'Getting Better'?

a. hesitant   b. purposeful   c. sluggish   d. frantic

2   Write the pitches of the first four bars of the bass guitar music. The first two notes are done for you:

3   Write the words of the first verse (up to 'rules'), then draw phrase marks (⌒) to show clearly the beginning and end of each phrase.

WHOLE SONG

4   The song begins with a drone formed by repeated notes. Later, this switches to the bass guitar. For how long does this drone last?

5 Write the melody that goes to the words 'Can't get no worse'. The first note has been done for you.

Can't

6 What sort of drums play immediately before the words 'I used to be cruel'?

7 Apart from the words, what differences are there between the first verse (from 'I used to get mad. . .' to '. . . your rules') and the third verse (from 'I used to be cruel. . .' to '. . .best that I can')?

8 In the third verse, how many beats' ***rest*** are there between 'loved' and 'man'? Write down this rest.

9 Name some of the ways in which this song uses repeats.

RESEARCH

1 Listen to some of The Beatles' songs. Are there any instruments which you would not normally expect to hear in rock music? If so, what are they, and how are they used?

2 Describe the music of any modern rock group, and show how they might have been influenced by the music of The Beatles.

3 Imagine that 'A Day in the Life' is being re-released as a single and that you have been asked to direct the video. Draw or describe some of the images you would use, and state exactly where they would come in the song.

TRY THIS

Rolled Gold by The Rolling Stones

'The Stones' were one of the other great rock groups of 'The Beatles' era, and this is a collection of their hit songs. The music is more obviously sensual and powerful than that of The Beatles, and to many people it seems more emotional. Listen to 'Satisfaction' or 'Honky Tonk Woman', and this quality, which rock musicians have described as 'funky', will hit you at once.

With The Beatles by The Beatles

All of The Beatles' LPs are worth listening to, but you may find it interesting to start with *With The Beatles*, which was made in 1963, and compare it with *Sgt. Pepper*. Even in their early days, when they recorded 'cover' versions of other people's songs, it is obvious that they were interested in such widely different styles as rock'n'roll, and Hollywood musicals. One of the best songs is probably 'All My Loving' with its wonderful descending bass lines and its vocal harmonies.

6 OSTINATO

Pac - Paca - Pac - Paca - Pac - Paca - Pac - Paca
shooka - shooka
ktuk-a tuka-tu...ka tuk

SYNCHRO SYSTEM
King Sunny Adé
and his African Beats

The music of black Africa is usually very rhythmic and exciting, and often uses *polyrhythms* – several different rhythms at a time – and *ostinatos* – rhythmic or melodic patterns which are repeated many times. Africans have invented many different instruments, and many varied styles of music. Much of this involves dancing and other expressive and visual arts. In Africa people do not usually just listen to the music – they join in by singing, playing or dancing.

In recent years, Western instruments have been used to create new styles of popular music which are a fusion of African folk music and Western rock music. King Sunny Adé is one of many African musicians to become popular in Europe and America as well as in Nigeria, where he was born.

COMPOSE

Compose a piece using ostinatos. You will need to work in a group of four to six people. Choose one instrument each, organised so that about half the group has untuned percussion instruments. The other half can use any melodic instruments that can play these notes: D, E, G, A, B, D¹, E¹.

or

FIRST choose one of the untuned percussion players to start. He or she makes a short rhythmic figure, and repeats it many times.

THEN each person in the group joins in one by one. Start with the untuned percussion players, and then involve the melodic instruments. As each person joins in, he or she makes a figure which *fits* well with the others, but is *different* from them. Let all the people in the group have plenty of time to make figures fit, and listen carefully to make sure that you all keep the beat together. These are your ostinatos, so when you are sure you have got them right, write them down.

NEXT each person makes a solo to fit with the ostinatos. Play the ostinatos as before, and let everyone in the group take a turn at being the soloist (soloists can sing to 'Ah' if they like). While you are the soloist you can try many different rhythms and, if you have a melodic instrument, different notes. Listen carefully to hear what fits best. While you are playing an ostinato, play very quietly, and listen to the soloist. Do this several times so that everyone has at least six turns at being the soloist.

FINALLY swap instruments so that those who had untuned instruments now have melodic ones. Then repeat all your instructions with new ostinatos and solos.

PERFORM

Perform your music to the rest of your class. As you listen to the others, decide how well the melodies fit the ostinatos.

LISTEN

Choose one of these rhythms, and select a suitable instrument to perform it (choose an instrument which will make a crisp, dry sound, such as a drum or woodblock):

When you can play it quite fast, listen to 'E Saiye Re' from *Synchro Sound*. Which rhythm is played by the **shekere**? Which is played by the bass drum? Which is played by the **agogo**?

Listen again, and play your rhythm in time with the music you hear.

Now play one of these melody lines on a melodic instrument, repeating it many times:

Learn to play it quite fast, then listen to 'E Saiye Re' again. Which melody is played by the bass, which by the lead, and which by the rhythm guitar?

Listen again, and play your melody in time with the music you hear.

Now listen to another track from the same recording as you do the following quiz.

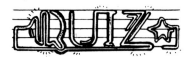

'Maajo'

FIRST VERSE

1 How many vocalists are there in the first verse?

2 What instruments accompany the vocalists?

3 In the chorus ('Maajo, maajo, maajo', etc.) are there
a. more   b. fewer   c. the same number of vocalists as in the verse?

SECOND VERSE TO THE END

4 How many times is the following ostinato played between the chorus and the second verse?

5 Does this ostinato   a. continue, or   b. stop when the second chorus is sung?

6 Describe what happens in the music immediately after this chorus.

7 Before the singing comes back, you will hear two short melodies. One is played on a synthesiser, and uses only two different notes. The other is played on an electric guitar, and uses three different notes. Which one is an ostinato?

8 What instrument plays a solo at the end of the song?

WHOLE SONG

9 Counting this solo as a *coda* (finishing section), write what you think is the form of this song. Let the verse be section A, the chorus section B, and different sections can be called C and D.

RESEARCH

1   Make a report about the music of black Africa. Find out as much as you can under the following headings:
    a. instruments
    b. singing styles (including '***call and response***')
    c. folk music
    d. pop music.

2   Discover how a 'talking drum' works. Why is it that some Africans can use their drums to talk to each other?

3   Find a song you like, and invent a rhythmic or melodic ostinato to fit to it. Perform it with its ostinato.

TRY THIS

Sounds d'Afrique

These are two recordings (*Sounds d'Afrique* and *Sounds d'Afrique 2*) which contain some of the best popular dance music of West Africa. Like Sunny Adé, the various musicians on these records use polyrhythms and ostinatos to form the basis of their music. Several of the tracks are in a style called 'high-life' which is clearly influenced by traditional jazz.

Missa Luba by Les Troubadours du Roi Bedouin

Most of this record consists of folk songs from what used to be called the Congo (now Zaïre), in energetic and spontaneous-sounding performances. Listen to 'Malingi Daba', a simple, tuneful song which has the heady atmosphere of a village celebration.

The *Missa Luba* itself was written by Fr. Guido Haazen, the Belgian priest who founded Les Troubadours. It is an effective and exciting blend of Congolese folk styles and Latin religious words.

7 MELODIES IN THIRDS

CARMINA BURANA
by Carl Orff

Carl Orff spent many years writing music in the style of other composers, including Arnold Schoenberg, before he worked out his own style, using strong, simple melodies and hypnotic repeating rhythms. He was involved in the theatre, and wanted his own music, including *Carmina Burana*, to be acted out dramatically at the same time as it was being performed musically.

He was deeply interested in music education, and evolved a whole new method of teaching music. He also invented a range of percussion instruments such as school xylophones and glockenspiels, which are still used today.

START

Play this melody using either two beaters on a *tuned percussion* instrument or a keyboard instrument.

To play this, you have to play two notes together. (Your teacher will show you how to do this.) In this piece, the two notes are always a *third* apart (see chapter 21 section 5).

Now try to play the same melody with each note a *fourth* apart:

And now with the notes a *fifth* apart:

When you have finished you can try with other intervals: a *second*, a *sixth*, a *seventh* or an *octave*. Compare the sounds of the different intervals. Which ones sound most discordant, or 'scrunchy'? Which ones sound most concordant or 'open'?

COMPOSE

Compose a piece which includes a melody in thirds.

○ FIRST make a quiet, mysterious beginning with a melody over a drone (see chapter 4).

○ NEXT make a more confident section with a melody in thirds. To do this make a short, interesting rhythmic figure, then use it to make:
some phrases which contain repeated notes,
some phrases in which every note moves by step,
some phrases which have leaps in the melody,
some phrases which have a confident feel to them.
Use some of these phrases, together with some ideas of your own, to make a middle section.

○ FINALLY make a loud, joyful ending for your piece. Practise it and write it down.

PERFORM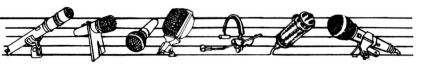

Perform your music to the rest of your class. As you listen to the others, decide what you can learn from each one.

LISTEN

Many composers have found melodies in thirds (when two notes are played together, a third apart) particularly effective. Listen to 'Fortune Plango Vulnera' from *Carmina Burana* by Carl Orff and raise your hand when you hear the music played and sung in thirds.

Listen again and play along with the melody in thirds (p. 39). Then listen to another movement from *Carmina Burana* as you do the following Quiz.

Dance from *Carmina Burana* by Carl Orff

FIRST THEME

1 Complete the following rhythm to match the rhythm of the notes you hear in bars 8, 9, 11, 12, 13 and 14:

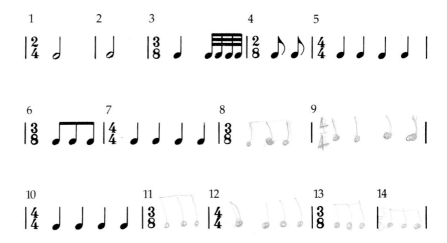

2 Name the instrument which plays on the second beat of bar 4.

3 Is the dynamic marking at the beginning *pp*, *mf* or *ff*?

4 Is the tempo marking presto, allegro, moderato or largo?

WHOLE PIECE

5 In which bar do the two solo violins start to play?

6 Do the solo violins play in thirds, fourths, fifths or sixths?

7 What musical device is used to accompany the two solo violins?

8 Which instrument accompanies the solo flute?

9 Is the melody immediately after the flute solo played by
   a. trumpets and horns
   b. horns and trombones
   c. trombones and tubas?

10 Counting the first four bars as an introduction, and using letters (A, B, C, etc.), write out the form of this music.

RESEARCH

1 Find out about the music of one of the following composers who lived at the same time as Carl Orff: Igor Stravinsky, Sergei Prokofiev, Arnold Schoenberg. Make a report for the rest of your class including where and when your composer lived, and describing at least one piece of his music.

2 Write out on a stave the approximate range of the following voices: *soprano*, *mezzo soprano*, *alto*, *counter-tenor*, *tenor*, *baritone*, *bass*.

3 Find out about the local choir(s) in your area. Where does it perform, how often does it rehearse, and what sort of music does it perform?

4 Find out about and write down three examples of the following intervals: a. *semitone* b. *tone* c. *major and minor intervals* d. augmented and diminished intervals e. perfect intervals (see chapter 21 section 5).

TRY THIS

Requiem by Fauré

CHOIR AND ORCHESTRA

Many people find it hard at first to listen to the sound of a choir and orchestra, because it is not always easy to distinguish the melodies from the general welter of sound. If you find it difficult to accustom your ears to the richness of these tone colours, try the *Requiem* by Fauré, and in particular the movement called 'Pie Jesu', which is written for a solo soprano. The words are from the *requiem* or Latin Mass for the Dead, but the music, far from being morbid, is serene and beautiful, and above all melodic.

Concerto for Orchestra by Bartók

ORCHESTRA

Concertos are really pieces for solo instruments with orchestral accompaniment, but in this piece almost every instrument has its own exciting solos to play. The second movement is a good example, with solos for pairs of instruments, each one separated by a different interval. Listen to it and you will hear bassoons playing their melody in sixths, then oboes playing their solo in thirds, clarinets in sevenths and so on.

8 SEMITONES AND WHOLE TONES

SYRINX by Debussy

Claude Debussy was one of the most original composers, with a style all of his own. Even as a student he shocked his teachers with his revolutionary ideas about harmony, and many later composers admired him for his futuristic way of composing.

Debussy was fascinated by the hazy, indistinct but glowing paintings which he saw at the 'Impressionist' painters' exhibitions, and he tried to create a similar impressionist atmosphere in his compositions. There is often a blurred, indistinct feel to his music, created by vague *tonality*, subtly shifting timbres and little snatches of melody. *Syrinx* is a typically quiet and subtle piece.

In most Western music (music where the style originates from Europe or America) the smallest interval is a semitone. Altogether there are twelve semitones in an octave:

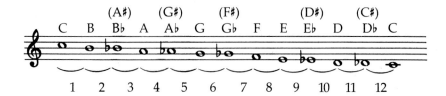

Play this melody from *Syrinx*. How many of the twelve semitones are included in it?

Now compare that melody, which is played at the beginning of *Syrinx*, with this from the end of *Syrinx*:

What do you notice?

In this music, Debussy uses several types of scale, including a **chromatic scale** (all the intervals are semitones) and a **whole tone scale** (all the intervals are tones).

chromatic scale

whole tone scale

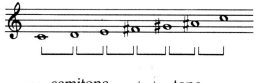

⌣ = semitone   ⊔ = tone

COMPOSE

Compose a piece for a solo instrument – any melodic instrument will do as long as it can play a chromatic scale.

○ FIRST construct the following:
Some phrases based on a whole tone scale.
Some phrases which use six or seven notes of a chromatic scale.
Some phrases which are repeated an octave higher (or lower).
Some fast, fluid phrases.
Some long, held notes.

○ THEN using some of these, together with some of your own ideas, make a piece that involves subtle changes in tempo (speed), dynamics (loudness) and mood.

○ FINALLY practise your music then write it down. If you cannot write it exactly do not worry – do the best you can to help you to remember your composition.

PERFORM

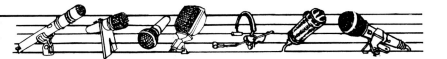

When you have finished and written your music, perform it to the rest of your class. As you listen to the others, try to hear when they use a chromatic scale and when they use a whole tone scale, and try to get a feeling of the flavour of each. Now listen to a performance of *Syrinx*.

Syrinx by Debussy

Explanation of terms

1 very moderate speed (slow)
3 a little faster (very little)
5 not in strict time
7 getting slower right up to the end
9 getting much slower

2 ritardando
4 slower
6 at original speed (very moderate)
8 marcato (give a little push to the beginning of the note)
10 dying away

Syrinx by Debussy

1 What instrument plays this music?

2 Look carefully at the music of the first two bars, then write the music of bar 3.

3 Draw four empty bars to represent the music for bars 4 to 8. Do not copy the notes, but underneath the stave write marks to show where the music gets louder (⧼) and softer (⧽).

4 What happens in the music at bar 9?

5 Fill in the rhythm of the music in bar 10, adding the phrase and dynamic marks.

6 Listen carefully to the music of bars 14 to 19. Where in the music does the player take a breath?

7 Complete the music of bar 15.

8 In bar 16 name the intervals
   a. between the first and second notes
   b. between the second and third notes
   c. between the fifth and sixth notes
   d. between the sixth and seventh notes.

9 Listen to the music in bars 23 and 24. What do you think the word 'trille' (*trill* in English) means?

10 Listen carefully to bars 29 and 30. In what ways are these bars
   a. similar to, and   b. different from the first bar of *Syrinx*?

11 Describe briefly how the music ends.

12 Which of these words does *not* describe the character of the music?
   a. vigorous   b. mysterious   c. majestic   d. haunting
   e. angry.

RESEARCH

1 Compose a piece of music for another solo instrument. Find out all you can about the instrument – what sort of music sounds most effective and what sort of 'character' the instrument has. Also find out its range, how loudly and how softly it can play, the effects it can produce, and whether it is a **transposing** instrument. Make your own music to suit the instrument.

2 Choose any instrument or voice and find out the names of any two of its most famous performers. Listen to one recording of each performer, and try to tell the differences between them. Hear how they communicate the character of the music by noticing the following things:
   a. their choice of tempo
   b. their use of contrasts
   c. the quality of their tone
   d. their attention to detail such as phrasing, attack, **legato**, **staccato** and dynamics.

3 Find and study some reproductions of paintings by the French Impressionist painters. How did they achieve their artistic effects? How did Debussy achieve his musical effects?

TRY THIS

'Prélude à l'Après-midi d'une Faune'

ORCHESTRA

The English title is 'Prelude to the Afternoon of a Faun'. It is a haunting and beautiful piece, typically Impressionist in its ever-changing orchestral colours. The atmosphere it portrays is sultry and lazy. Listen for the main **theme**, which is based on a chromatic scale, and is very similar to the opening of *Syrinx*.

'The Girl with the Flaxen Hair' ('La Fille aux Cheveux de Lin')

PIANO

The atmosphere of this short piece is much cooler and simpler, but still very sensitive. Try, if you are a pianist, to play through some of the music (it should be obtainable from main libraries). It is difficult to perform, but playing through sections will give you a good basis for listening to a performance. It comes from Debussy's first book of *Préludes*, and it is worth listening to some other **preludes** from the same book, in particular 'The Sunken Cathedral' (La Cathédrale Engloutie') and to 'Veils' ('Voiles'), which uses a whole tone scale.

9 MAJOR AND MINOR

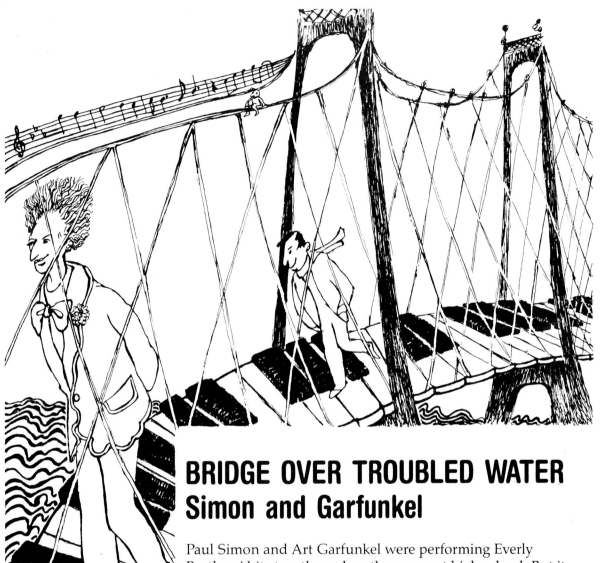

BRIDGE OVER TROUBLED WATER
Simon and Garfunkel

Paul Simon and Art Garfunkel were performing Everly Brothers' hits together when they were at high school. But it was not until they had left school, started separate careers, and then got back together again that they started to sing the music that would make them famous.

Their voices blended perfectly, and their songs, which were highly sophisticated, had the seemingly spontaneous quality of fine poetry. They made only a handful of recordings together before going their separate ways, but these are still an inspiration to many people.

START

As you know, most of the music that people hear around them is not based on the chromatic scale or the whole tone scale. Most of the music you hear is probably based on a scale which has a mixture of tones and semitones – a *major* or *minor scale*.

Make a major scale. You do it like this:
a. Choose any note to be your keynote.
b. Start on that note, then go up by the following intervals: tone, tone, semitone, tone, tone, tone, semitone.

You should have ended up exactly an octave above your starting note. Did you?

Now choose C as your keynote, and play a C major scale. Practise it until you can play it without hesitations, and listen to the sound that the major scale makes. How many sharps or flats did you play?

Now play the following scales:
G major (keynote G)   B♭ major (keynote B♭)
F major (keynote F)   F♯ major (keynote F♯)

Which sharps or flats do you play in each of these scales?

PERFORM

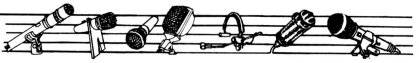

Perform 'Bye Bye Love'. This uses notes which are almost entirely in the major scale, i.e. it is in a *major key*.

Now play the same melody, but with the following changes:
Instead of B play B♭
Instead of E play E♭
Instead of F♯ play F

These three changes mean that 'Bye Bye Love' is no longer in a major key. It is in a *minor key*.

Make a minor scale like this:
a. Choose any note to be your keynote.
b. Start on the keynote, and go up by the following intervals: tone, semitone, tone, tone, semitone, tone, tone.

You should have ended up exactly an octave above your starting note; i.e. on your keynote again. Did you?

Now play the following scales:
A minor (keynote A)   B minor (keynote B)
E minor (keynote E)   G minor (keynote G)

Bye Bye Love

Melody: Bye bye love. Bye bye hap-pin-ess / sweet ca-ress

Hel - lo lone - li - ness__ I think I'm goin' to / feel like I could

1.G cry ___ 2.G die ___ Bye bye my love, good bye ___

1. There goes my ba - by ___ with some-one new,

She sure looks hap - py ___ I sure am blue ___

She was my ba - by ___ till he stepped in.

Good - bye to ro - mance that might have bin.

2. I'm through with romance I'm through with love
I'm through with countin' the stars above
And here's the reason that I'm so free
My love, my baby is through with me.

COMPOSE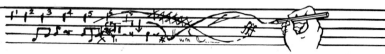

Compose a piece of music which contrasts major and minor keys. You will need any melodic instrument.

○ FIRST make a melody using the notes of a G minor scale. If you like, you can use the instructions in the Compose section of chapter 2. You can also use drones, ostinatos and melodies in thirds.

○ NEXT play the same melody using the notes of a G major scale. If you like, you can help the character of the music to change by playing it faster, or quieter, more assertively or more joyfully.

○ THEN arrange the two sections of your music in a way that sounds good to you. Try the following:
some phrases played in the major key and repeated in the minor;
some parts of major key phrases repeated in the minor;
the whole melody played in the major key and repeated in the minor.

○ FINALLY practise your music and write it down. Keep this music – you will use it again in chapter 20.

PERFORM

Perform your music to the rest of your class. As you listen to the others, try to hear the shifts from the major key to the minor key.

LISTEN

Listen to 'Bye Bye Love' and 'El Condor Pasa', to appreciate the different flavours of the major and minor keys.

Apart from the difference in tonality, what other contrasts are there between these songs?

'The Boxer' by Simon and Garfunkel

1 Is this song in a major or a minor key?

2 Briefly describe the character of the song.

3 Write the pitch of the four bass notes that are played by the guitar during the introduction. The first note has been done for you:

8ve

4 What are the words when the singing splits into harmony?

5 Which of the following rhythms is played by the drum?

A

B

C

6 Copy the words to the second verse (below), and draw phrase marks (‿) to show clearly how the vocalists phrase their music (i.e. how much they sing to each breath).

When I left my home and my family
I was no more than a boy,
In the company of strangers,
In the quiet of the railway station,
Running scared; laying low;
Seeking out the poorer quarters
Where the ragged people go;
Looking for the places only they would know.

7 Is the chorus sung   a. mainly in thirds   b. mainly in fifths or   c. mainly in sixths?

8 Fill in the missing notes of the synthesiser's melody:

9 Write out the form of this song using the following words:
introduction, verse, chorus, instrumental break, coda.

RESEARCH

1 Learn about scales and key signatures (see chapter 21 sections 6 and 7). Then take any songbook which contains music as well as words, and find

a. five songs which start on the tonic
b. five songs which start on the dominant
c. three songs which start on a different degree of the scale (name the degrees).

Then choose any song that you do not already know, and go through it, deciding on which degree of the scale each note comes. Finally, without using an instrument, learn to sing the song. How can your knowledge of scales help you to do this?

2 Choose any song you know which is in a major key, and perform it in the minor. What difference does this make to the character of the music?

3 Choose three pieces of music you know. Listen to them, and decide whether they are in major or minor keys. Choose from this list:

'La Mourisque'   by Susato
'Love Me Tender'   by Elvis Presley
'E Saiye Re'   by King Sunny Adé
Symphony No. 5   by Beethoven
'Fortune Plango Vulnera' by Carl Orff

TRY THIS

Graceland by Paul Simon

After Simon and Garfunkel split up, they continued to perform separately, and one of the best records that either has produced is probably *Graceland*. It is heavily influenced by African music, and contains some fine performances by black South African musicians. Listen to the rich vocal harmonies in 'Homeless', or the wonderful way in which the ostinatos blend with the melody in 'Under African Skies', or the driving beat of 'That was your Mother'.

Blue by Joni Mitchell

Joni Mitchell, like Simon and Garfunkel, performed in a style that was influenced by folk music. Although much of the music in this style was very simple, her own music is rewarding and complex, with wide intervals, long spaced-out phrases and unusual harmonies. The title track ('Blue') is particularly evocative.

10 VARIATIONS

THE YOUNG PERSON'S GUIDE TO THE ORCHESTRA
by Benjamin Britten

Benjamin Britten was one of the greatest English composers of this century. His music is based on the styles that were popular at the end of the nineteenth century, but the wide melodic intervals, spiky harmonies and speech-like rhythms give it a much more modern flavour. He was fascinated by traditional Japanese music, and for a time every piece he composed seemed to have a Japanese influence.

Like Carl Orff, Britten was interested in music education, and wrote *The Young Person's Guide to the Orchestra* as a musical explanation of what an orchestra is, and the original performance incorporated a spoken introduction to each instrument. It is also called 'Variations and Fugue on a Theme of Purcell'.

START

Play this melody by Purcell:

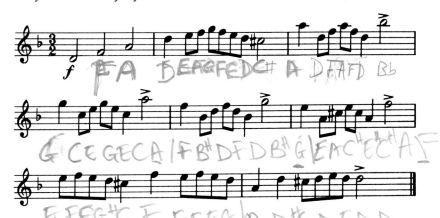

Now go through it, naming all the intervals. What do you notice about bars 3 to 6?

LISTEN

Listen to the beginning of 'Variations and Fugue on a Theme of Purcell'. You will hear how Britten arranged this melody for orchestra. Then, after a short link, you will hear what appears to be the same melody, played again.

As you listen, follow the music printed above. What did you notice?

You probably heard that the second melody is different from the first. Did you hear what the differences are?

This effect, of being similar but different, is called **variation**.

Listen to the next variation, following Purcell's melody. See if you can spot the differences between the melody of this variation and that of Purcell's theme.

Now do the same for the next two variations. Listen carefully and try to spot all the differences. You should find examples of these:

    using different tone colours
    using different keys
    leaving out notes or groups of notes
    having figures played upside-down (*inverted*)
    having figures played backwards (*retrograde*)

changing the rhythm of a figure

having a figure played higher (or lower) than it is played in the theme

This effect, of having a theme performed several times, but each time with new alterations to it, is called 'theme and variations', or 'variation form'.

Variation form

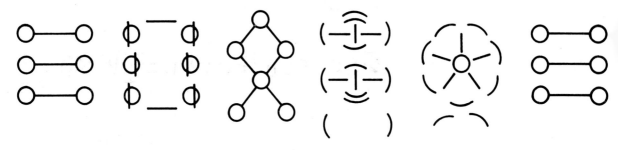

COMPOSE

Now that you know how Britten made some variations, you can make some of your own. Use the theme below. You will need at least two instruments – one must be melodic, and one must be an untuned percussion instrument. If you like you can work with a partner but you should try to make at least three variations each.

Theme by Nick Barlow

○ FIRST practise the theme until you can play it without pauses or hesitations.

○ THEN make your variations. (Remember, Britten varied the theme by Purcell in all the ways listed on pp. 57–8). You can use some of the same techniques to make your composition. As soon as you have finished one variation, write it down.

○ FINALLY put your theme and variations together in the same way as Britten did.
First play the theme, then all the variations, and then repeat the theme.
Listen carefully and choose the best order for playing the variations.

PERFORM

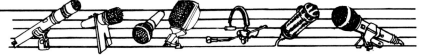

Perform your theme and variations to the rest of your class.

As you listen to the others, see if you can discover how their variations relate to the theme.

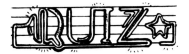

The Young Person's Guide to the Orchestra by Britten (Variation J to the end)

VARIATION J

1 What is the interval with which the horns' variation begins?

2 At the start of this variation the strings are marked 'trem. pont.'. What is this short for, what does it mean, and what effect does it have on the sound?

VARIATION K

3 Write the rhythm that is played by the side-drum during the trumpets' variation.

VARIATION L

4 Copy the melody that begins the trombones' variation (below). Write the rhythm of the *accompaniment* above the stave.

5 What part of Purcell's theme is used in this melody? How is it varied?

VARIATION M

6 Name the solo percussion instruments, and the order in which they appear during the percussion variation.

FUGUE

7 The following instruments play the melody of the fugue. Write them out in the order in which you hear them:

violas	oboes	horns	xylophone/timpani
bassoons	clarinets	cellos	double basses
harp	trumpets	violin I	trombones and tuba
violin II	piccolo	flutes	

8 Describe how the character of the music changes from the beginning of the fugue to the end.

VARIATION J TO THE END

9 Match each variation with its correct *time signature*:

Variation J $\frac{2}{4}$ Variation L $\frac{3}{2}$

Variation K $\frac{6}{8}$ Variation M $\frac{4}{4}$

10 What are the differences between the theme as it is played at the beginning of the music and the theme as it is played at the end?

RESEARCH

1 Find out about the music of the following British composers: Ralph Vaughan Williams, Sir Michael Tippett, Sir Peter Maxwell Davies. Find out what their main compositions are, and describe *one* composition by one of them.

2 Look at the list of instruments in question 7 above. For each instrument, find out the following:

a. how its sounds are made.
b. its *range*
c. its *clef*(s)
d. if and how its music is transposed.
e. whether it uses any special techniques such as *pizzicato*.

3   Listen to one of the following sets of variations. How does the composer vary the theme?

    a. *Variations on 'America'* by Ives
    b. *Variations on a Nursery Tune* by Dohnanyi
    c. *Variations on a Rococo Theme* by Tchaikovsky
    d. *Variations on a Theme by Paganini* by Rachmaninov
    e. *Variations* by Lloyd-Webber.

4   Describe what a **fugue** is, and explain what is meant by the following terms: **subject**, counter-subject, **stretto**, **episode**, **diminution**, augmentation.

TRY THIS

Four 'Sea Interludes' from *Peter Grimes* by Britten

ORCHESTRA

These short **interludes** come from Britten's **opera** *Peter Grimes* and are all intended to represent different moods of the sea. They are very dramatic, and the music really does seem to evoke the sort of feelings people associate with the sea – cold waves lapping on the shore in one interlude, angry breakers crashing in another. The titles are 'Dawn', 'Sunday Morning', 'Moonlight' and 'Storm'. If you get a chance (and you can afford it) try to see the whole of *Peter Grimes*. It is a genuinely moving opera, with a simple but profound plot, realistic characters and dramatic music.

Serenade for tenor, horn and strings by Britten

This is an evocative set of songs. Each one is different, but put together they make a well-integrated piece of music. Listen to 'This Aye Nighte', where the tenor sings the same melody over and over above a gradual, exciting **crescendo** and **diminuendo** in the instrumental parts. The haunting horn solo which begins and ends the serenade is played without pressing down the **valves**, as if it were a hunting horn or a bugle.

11 CHORDS

SYMPHONY NO. 9 'FROM THE NEW WORLD' by Dvořák

Anton Dvořák came from a country called Bohemia (now called Czechoslovakia). He had a great love for his homeland which was not at that time independent, and like many other **Nationalist** composers he tried to put the spirit of his country into his music. One of the ways he did this was by incorporating folk music rhythms, forms and melodic styles into his compositions.

Dvořák's music is particularly tuneful, even in his most serious pieces, and he makes good use of the energetic rhythms of Czech folk dances. His Ninth Symphony, 'From the New World', was written in America, where he spent three years and became fascinated by the music of the American blacks.

START

A *chord* is what you get when you play several notes simultaneously. The most common chord can be played like this.

Take the scale of C major. Starting with C, play a note, miss one, play a note, miss one, then play one:

You now have a chord of C major:

Try the following. Using any instrument on which you can play three notes at once, play these chords:

| F | A | D | E minor | G minor |

Now make six other chords in the same way.

Sometimes composers use just three notes sounding together. More often, however, they use four, five or even more notes sounding together. The most common way of adding these extra notes (and so making the sound 'fatter') is to 'double' the notes already in the chord by making them sound at different octaves. For example, a chord like this:

might be changed to something like this:

or this:    or this:

How many other ways can you find of playing this chord?

Play these chords:

E   B♭   E   C♯   A   F♯m   C♯

When you have the sound of these chords firmly in your head, play these:

In what way are they similar to the chords you have already played?

Listen to the beginning of the Second Movement of the Symphony No. 9 by Dvořák. In this music Dvořák uses these chords (in a different key) as a sort of frame. In the middle of the frame, like the middle section of a ternary form piece, he puts a slow, quiet melody, played by a *cor anglais*.

Compare the chords you have heard with this music, played by the clarinets a little later:

In this music, the notes of the chord are not played together, but one after another. This musical pattern (having the notes of a chord played one after another) is called an ***arpeggio***.

COMPOSE

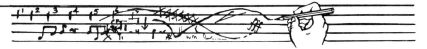

Make a set of variations based on a progression of chords. You will need a keyboard instrument or a tuned percussion instrument.

○ FIRST decide which chords you are going to use. Choose five to eight chords (major or minor), and experiment by putting them in different orders until you find some that sound good together. Then write them down.

○ NEXT find different ways of playing your chords. Make the following:
Some variations which use only arpeggios.
Some variations which alternate arpeggios and block chords.
Some variations which alternate thin and thick textures.
Some variations which sound delicate.
Some variations which sound flowing.
Some variations which use repeated notes to give a sense of urgency.

○ FINALLY practise your music and write it down. If you find it difficult to write the whole composition, try to get at least the first bar of each variation written correctly.

PERFORM

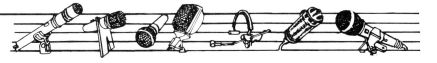

Perform your music to the rest of your class. As you listen to the others, decide which variations sound smooth, and which sound more jagged. What makes them sound smooth or jagged?

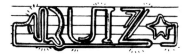

Symphony No. 9 'From the New World' (Second Movement)

SECTION A
FIRST PLAYING

1   Play this melody. It is the same as the melody which the cor anglais plays, but contains mistakes. Can you spot the wrong notes?

SECOND PLAYING

2   What instrument enters on the last chord of the chord sequence which begins this movement?

3   After the chord sequence has been repeated, the violins and cellos play. Do they play   a. in thirds   b. in fifths   c. in sixths or   d. in octaves?

4   Which instruments echo the cor anglais when it re-appears?

THIRD PLAYING

5   Here is the music which is played by the first horn immediately before the next section begins. Copy it out, and write in the second horn's music underneath. The first bar has been done for you.

SECTION B

FIRST PLAYING

6   Which two instruments play the melody at the beginning of this section?

7   Which instruments are played pizzicato during this section?

8 The following music is played immediately after the pizzicato.
Name the instruments A, B, C, D and E.

THE WHOLE MOVEMENT

9 Describe some of the differences in character between sections
A and B.

10 Which of the following statements is correct?

    a. Section A is minor and section B is major.
    b. Section A is major and section B is minor.
    c. Both sections are in major keys.
    d. Both sections are in minor keys.

11 Describe the music between the repeat of the cor anglais solo and the end of the movement.

RESEARCH

1 Find out about the music of one of the following Nationalist composers: Smetana, Greig, Sibelius, Mussorgsky. Make a report for the rest of your class which includes
    a. where and when your composer lived
    b. the main events in his life
    c. a detailed description of *one* of his compositions.

2 Find out how to write chords   a. in close position, and b. for four-part choir.   Then write out the following chords in both ways: C, F, Bb, Eb, G, D, A.

3 The music that fascinated Dvořák was the music of the spirituals. Find out about spirituals. Many songbooks contain one or two – learn one so that you can perform it.

TRY THIS

Slavonic Dance No. 8 by Dvořák

ORCHESTRA

This is in the style of a *furiant*, a swaggering Czech folk dance. It has all the energy of a folk dance, but is really much more sophisticated. Dvořák gives us sudden changes in dynamics, moves swiftly between major and minor tonalities, and has rhythms in twos against rhythms in threes. It is an exciting orchestral showpiece.

Cello Concerto in B minor by Dvořák

CELLO AND ORCHESTRA

This concerto is a really rich, lush **Romantic** piece, brimming with heart-rending melodies and emotional outpourings. It is also many people's idea of typical cello music. Start by getting to know the last movement.

12 MORE ABOUT CHORDS

SYMPHONY NO. 94 IN G 'THE SURPRISE' by Haydn

Franz Joseph Haydn was, with Mozart, one of the greatest composers of the classical times. His music does not usually have the heart-searching emotion that people find in Mozart's, but it often conveys such cheerful happiness that it makes people feel good to listen to it.

Although Haydn wrote his music strictly in the classical style, he was an imaginative composer, and his music is never obvious. Loud and stormy sections often stop in mid-flow, and there are unusual harmonies, uneven melodies and the occasional sudden silence. The 'surprise' in the title of this symphony is the extra-loud chord in the second movement, but it is fair to say that Haydn's music is full of such surprises.

START

Many melodies use the notes of a common chord or ***triad*** side by side. Melodies which do this are often strong and memorable, and you can usually tell what the harmonies are just by singing or playing the melody.

For instance, play these phrases which are based on a C major chord:

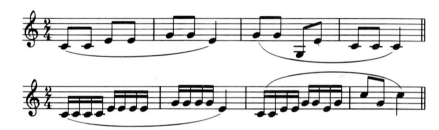

Now construct some more melodic phrases based on a C major chord.

Many melodies, of course, are based on two or more chords. Play these examples which are based on the chords C and G7:

(For an explanation of 7th chords, see chapter 21 section 10.)

COMPOSE

Compose a melody based on chords.

○ FIRST choose two or maybe three chords which fit well together.

○ NEXT make the following:
Some phrases which use the pitches of only one chord.
Some phrases in which the pitches go up through one chord and down through another.
Some phrases which use repeated pitches.
Some phrases which contain wide leaps.

○ FINALLY choose some of these, together with some of your own ideas, to make your melody. If you like, you can harmonise your melody by playing both the melody and the chords at the same time.

Listen to the theme from the second movement of 'The Surprise' Symphony by Haydn. As you listen, follow the melody (below).

Look at Haydn's melody. Which phrases are made up out of the notes of a triad? Which phrases are made up out of other notes?

You can probably find many 'extra' notes in the melody. For instance, instead of writing this:

chord notes

Haydn writes this:

extra notes

These extra notes do not really fit the chord they go with, but they still sound right. This is because

a. each one comes next to a chord note, and
b. each one is only a tone (or a semitone) away from that chord note.

Play the melody you have composed once more, and this time add some extra notes. Listen carefully to check whether or not you like the effect they have on your melody.

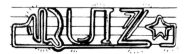

Symphony No. 94 in G 'The Surprise' (Second Movement, Theme and Variations)

THEME

1   Write out the first four bars of the theme, and write staccato dots (·) under the notes which are played staccato.

2   Which instruments play pizzicato, and in which bars?

VARIATION 1

3 Which instruments play the *counter-melody*?

4 Listen out for this counter-melody and fill in the gaps in bar 4, bar 7, bar 10 and bar 14:

VARIATION 2

5 Which of the following statements is true?

   a. The first half of this variation starts in unison and continues in harmony.
   b. The first half of this variation starts in harmony and continues in unison.
   c. The first half of this variation is in unison throughout.
   d. The first half of this variation is in harmony throughout.

6 How many times do you hear the following scale pattern?

VARIATION 3

7 What is the solo instrument at the beginning of this variation?

8 Listen carefully for this music. Where exactly do you hear discords?

VARIATION 4

9 Name some of the ways in which the middle two sections of this variation are different from the outer two sections (the form is A A B B).

CODA

10 What musical device do you hear at the beginning of the coda?

11 When the first four bars of the theme are repeated at the end of the movement, is the harmony

    a. the same as at the beginning?
    b. very similar to the beginning?
    c. completely different from the beginning?

THE WHOLE MOVEMENT

12 Which variations are in a major key, and which in the minor?

RESEARCH

1 Find out the difference between major and minor chords (see chapter 21 section 8). Starting on any note, play a major scale, and then play the triads which are built on these notes. How many of your triads are major, how many are minor and how many are neither major nor minor?

2   Choose a song to perform, preferably with its harmony. As you practise it, decide

a. which melody notes are also notes of the chord, and
b. which melody notes are extra notes.

3   Find and study some photographs of eighteenth-century architecture (e.g. by Christopher Wren) and paintings (e.g. by Reynolds and Gainsborough). Do you think that there are any elements in the style of eighteenth-century art which are reflected in the music of Haydn and Mozart?

TRY THIS

The Creation by Haydn
SOLO SINGERS, CHOIR AND ORCHESTRA
This is an **oratorio**, with beautiful and tuneful **arias** and colourful **recitatives**, all based on the bible story of the creation of the world. Typically imaginative moments include the portrayal of rain, snow, the sun rising, various animals, and an amazing representation of chaos. This has repeated chords and little wisps of melody, and is unlike anything else from classical times. Listen for a typical Haydn surprise near the beginning of *The Creation* when the choir sings 'and there was light'.

The 'Emperor' Quartet by Haydn
STRING QUARTET
This piece is one of many great string quartets by Haydn. The slow movement is a famous theme and variations, based on a theme that is so stately and dignified that it is now the Austrian national anthem. The first and last movements are both cheerful and lively, and the third movement is a vigorous **minuet**.

13 MUSIC AND WORDS

Are you going to Scarborough Fair?

BYKER HILL
Martin Carthy

Before radio became popular, the music many people heard was folk music. All around the world, when village communities had something to celebrate, their amateur musicians would perform the music they had learned by heart, and the people would eat, drink, sing and dance and have a good time. But not all folk music was happy. Farm labourers sang at their back-breaking work; soldiers sang, marching to war and perhaps death; tired-out sailors kept their spirits up with music.

By the end of the nineteenth century, this way of life was rapidly dying, particularly in Europe and North America, and its rich and varied music was almost forgotten. But in many countries small groups of enthusiasts travelled around recording and writing down all the folk music people could remember. This music, along with modern songs in folk music style, is kept alive today, performed at folk clubs, festivals, *ceilidhs* and even in the streets by artists like Martin Carthy.

START

Read these words, which have been used as song lyrics:

What did the wife of the soldier get
From the ancient city of Prague?
From Prague she got the linen shirt
It matched her skirt, did the linen shirt
That she got from the city of Prague.

What did the wife of the soldier get
From Brussels, the Belgian town?
From Brussels she got the delicate lace
Oh, the charm and the grace of the delicate lace
That she got from the Belgian town.

What did the wife of the soldier get
From Paris, the city of light?
From Paris she got the silken dress
Oh, to possess the silken dress
That she got from the city of light.

What did the wife of the soldier get
From Libya's desert sands?
From Libya she got the little charm
Around her arm she wore the charm
That she got from the desert sands.

What did the wife of the soldier get
From Russia's distant steppes?
From Russia she got the widow's veil
And the end of the tale is the widow's veil
That she got from the distant steppes.

'The Wife of the Soldier' by Bertolt Brecht

What is the story behind the words?

What do you think is the mood of the words?

How can the feelings behind the words be brought out by the
way the song is   a. composed, and   b. performed?

COMPOSE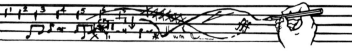

Construct a piece of music using the words to 'The Wife of the Soldier'. An instrument is not essential. You can compose a song, or background music to the spoken words.

○ FIRST decide on the overall character of your piece. To do this, read the lyrics again. Can you make them sound
a. innocent and joky   b. bitter   c. mocking?

When you have done that, think about a vocal style that will help to communicate the character you have decided on. Also decide which instruments, if any, you would like to use.

○ NEXT think about the form of the piece you want to create. Will each verse be the same? Will there be an introduction or a coda? What sort of repeats will you use?

○ THEN make the following:
Some phrases which use repeated notes.
Some phrases which use notes of a chromatic scale.
Some phrases which use notes of a chord.
Some phrases which contain a mixture of steps and leaps.

Use some of the phrases that you make, in a way that will communicate the character of your piece, and then construct your music.

○ FINALLY practise it and write it down.

PERFORM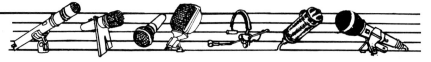

Perform your piece to the rest of your class. As you listen to the others, decide which piece is most dramatic, and whether the most dramatic pieces are the most effective.

LISTEN

Listen to 'The Wife of the Soldier'. How does Martin Carthy's version compare with those of your class?

'Lucy Wan'

THE WORDS

1 Why is Lucy Wan 'weeping and making moan'?

2 How does her brother kill her?

3 What reasons does Geordie give for the blood?

4 What, at the end of the song, is Geordie going to do?

5 How are the feelings in the song communicated by the way in which it is performed?

THE MUSIC

6 Complete the music of the first phrase:

Fair Lu - cy she sits at her father's door

7 In the second verse, what are the *intervals* between
a. 'ill' and 'tell'?
b. 'for' and 'there'?
c. 'brother' and 'and'?

8 In the fourth verse, which of the following words is *ornamented*?
'And he is away to his mother's house,'
'What ails thee, Geordie Wan?'

9 Write a *graphic score* of the last verse, showing clearly the number of notes to each word, the approximate length and pitch of each note, and any ornaments that are used. You will need to write the words beneath your graphic symbols.

10 This song uses a *mode* different from major and minor scales. Write out all the notes of the mode used in this song.

RESEARCH

1 Choose one of the following folk traditions, and make a report about it to the rest of your class:

morris, clog or sword dances
folk tales
nursery rhymes with hidden meanings
mummers' plays

2   Find out about some of the songs, tales and traditions that come from your part of the world. Think about traditions associated with particular times of the year: May Day, Hallowe'en, Shrove Tuesday, etc. Are any of these kept alive today?

3   Listen to these pieces of vocal music, and compare the styles of singing that you hear. Think about tone, phrasing, dynamics, colouring, range and other expressive qualities. Choose from this list:
'Love Me Tender' (chapter 2)
Mother India (chapter 4)
'A Day in the Life' (chapter 5)
'Fortune Plango Vulnera' (chapter 7)
'Lucy Wan' (chapter 13)

TRY THIS

Music by The Chieftans

The Chieftans are an internationally famous Irish band. They have made many fine recordings, including *The Chieftans Live* which has the usual heady mix of energetic **reels** and **jigs** and the exciting atmosphere of a 'live' concert. Listen to 'Carrick Fergus' which starts as a harp solo, is a slow, sentimental **air**, and is particularly haunting. Most of the rest of the music is dance music, and is breathtaking in its vigour and rhythmic drive.

Music by Steeleye Span

Steeleye Span have described themselves as 'a rock band which happens to play folk music'. Much of their music is probably closer to rock – they play electric instruments – but their roots are in traditional folk music (Martin Carthy was a member for some time). One of their best recordings is *Below the Salt* which contains several magnificent tracks, in particular 'King Henry'. Listen especially to the commanding performances of the lead singer, Maddy Prior.

Music by your local folk groups

Folk music is still cherished by many people, and there are thousands of solo singers and groups. Only some of these are recorded, but many fine and moving performances can be heard at traditional folk clubs. There is probably one within a few miles of your home.

14 USING TWO CHORDS

RASTAMAN VIBRATION
BOB MARLEY AND THE WAILERS

The *reggae* style was born in Jamaica in the late 1960s, and is now popular worldwide. Its roots go back to African music, but what may strike you most about it is the bass which plays its *riffs* very loud, and the beat which has its *accents* on the second and fourth beats of every bar.

Many reggae songs are connected with the Rasta religion. Rastas believe that Ethiopia is their true homeland, to which they will one day return. In the meantime they live in exile, in 'Babylon'.

Bob Marley and the Wailers are probably the most famous of all reggae groups. Their music is slicker and more professionally produced than most, and they have done more than anyone to make reggae popular throughout the world. Bob Marley died of cancer in 1981, but the music of the Wailers lives on.

START

Play this music:

chords

riff

LISTEN

When you can play this music without hesitations, listen to 'Crazy Baldheads' by Bob Marley and the Wailers. How many times do you hear the riff you have played? Listen again and raise your hand a. when the chords stop playing, and b. when they re-start. Also listen to find out what the words are about. Listen once more, and play your riff and chords together with Bob Marley and the Wailers. Listen very carefully, and be sure to keep in time with the recording.

COMPOSE

Compose a piece based on two chords. You will need one instrument that can play chords and an untuned percussion instrument.

○ FIRST choose your two chords. To understand the effect that a change of chords can have, play the following, repeating each one several times:
4 bars of one chord, then 4 bars of the other;
12 bars of one chord, then 4 bars of the other;
8½ bars of one chord, then 3½ bars of the other.

○ THEN make a riff to fit the chords. Practise playing the riff and the chords together, and try to make the chord changes sound unexpected.

○ NEXT it is a good idea to record the background of your music, which you have just made, either on tape, or by writing it down. Now make the foreground of the music, either by singing or playing phrases which fit the chords. Make the following:

Some phrases that use repeated notes.
Some phrases that use just the notes of the chords.
Some phrases that use extra notes.
Some phrases that include rests.
Some rhythmic phrases which are played on an untuned instrument.

○ FINALLY try many different phrases and choose the ones you like best to make a piece in reggae or rock music style. If you need help to perform your music, ask your teacher or a friend. If you have a multi-track tape recorder available, you might like to add a drum track.

PERFORM

Perform your music to the rest of your class. As you listen to the others, decide how well the melodies, chords and riffs all fit together.

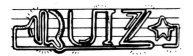

'War' by Bob Marley and the Wailers

The lyrics of this song are from a speech by the late Emperor Haile Selassie of Ethiopia.

FIRST PLAYING

1 How many times do you hear this riff in 'War'?

2 Which note in this riff is not part of the chord?

SECOND PLAYING

3 Which instrument plays repeated chords?

4 Listen for this music. Is it   a. a drone   b. a riff
c. a melody, or   d. a chord?

THIRD PLAYING

5   Listen for the chord that the backing group sings to the word 'War'. Is it   a. major   b. minor, or   c. neither major nor minor?

6   Listen for this melody. How many times is it played?

FOURTH PLAYING

7   Write the music that is sung to the following words (the first note has been done for you):

8   Name some of the ways in which this song uses repeats.

FIFTH PLAYING

9   Briefly describe the meaning of the lyrics.

10   How well do you think the lyrics fit to the riffs and the chords? Are there any places where they do not match well?

RESEARCH

1 Find out about these *cadences*: perfect, imperfect, plagal, interrupted (chapter 21 section 9 will help). Then learn how to play each cadence in three different keys. Finally choose a song you would like to perform and, as you practise it, decide where the cadences come. How will this knowledge affect your performance?

2 Choose one of the following musical styles, all from the Caribbean: mento, *steel band*, ska, calypso, soca. Then listen to two or three pieces of music in that style. What are the main differences between those pieces and the songs on *Rastaman Vibration*?

3 Choose one of the following and make a short report about it for the rest of your class: Jamaican food, Jamaican festivals, Anancy stories, Rastafarian beliefs.

TRY THIS

Reggae Greats by Toots and the Maytals

Toots Hibbert sings an early version of reggae called *rock steady*, and this LP shows an amazing variety of music within this style, including a reggae version of John Denver's famous song 'Country Roads'. Several tracks show how you can build a satisfying song using just two chords. Listen to 'Time Tough', and you can play along using chords F and C. Other two-chord songs are 'Bam Bam' which uses D and A7, and '54–46' which uses G and C.

Signing Off by UB40

UB40 is a British reggae band, whose style is very different from that of Bob Marley and the Wailers. Listening to their music you will still hear bass guitar riffs and organ chords, but it may be the haunting saxophone melodies and the electronic echoes that stay in your mind the longest. *Signing Off* is an excellent example of this style, and is heavy with reggae atmosphere.

15 CHORDS IN TRIPLE TIME

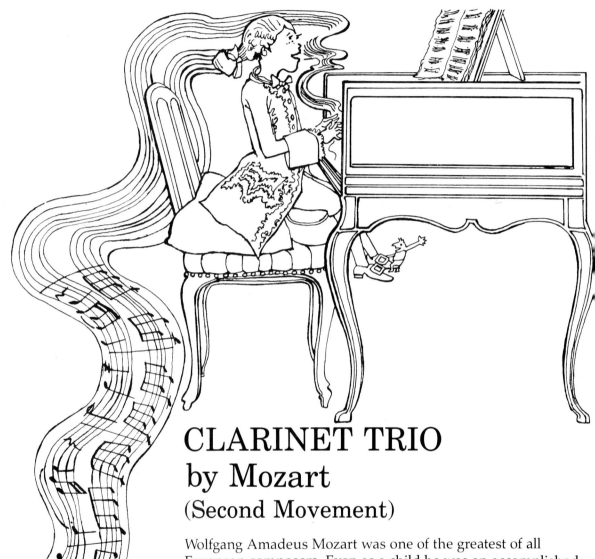

CLARINET TRIO
by Mozart
(Second Movement)

Wolfgang Amadeus Mozart was one of the greatest of all European composers. Even as a child he was an accomplished and famous pianist, and he had written over a hundred pieces of music by the time he was 11.

Mozart's music is written in the Classical style – elegant, stylish and refined – but it is generally more profound and more dramatic than most other music of the Classical time. People have tried to describe the effect of his music in words, talking of 'joy tinged with inexpressible sadness' and other such phrases, but you can only feel this effect by listening to his music.

The clarinet at that time was a new instrument and Mozart loved the rich range of tone colours it could produce. He wrote his Clarinet Trio for Anton Stadler, a famous clarinettist who was a friend of his.

START

It is likely that most of the music you listen to and compose has a beat. Probably for most of this music, the beat is in **quadruple** (or four) *time*. To see if a piece of music is in four time, try this test:

1   While the music is being played, find the beat.

2   Try saying '1, 2, 3, 4, 1, 2, 3, 4', etc. in time with the beat.

If this fits the beat of the music, then it is in four time.

LISTEN

Try this with some of the music you have already heard.
Listen very carefully to hear the beat. Tap in time with the beat.
Then count '1, 2, 3, 4, 1, 2, 3, 4' etc. in time with your tapping.
Choose two or three pieces from this list:

'Pavane La Bataille'   by Susato
'Heartbreak Hotel'   by Elvis Presley
'Getting Better'   by The Beatles
'E Saiye Re'   by King Sunny Adé
'The Boxer'   by Simon and Garfunkel

Do you hear the quadruple-time beat?

Some music is in three time, called **triple time**. In triple time you can count '1, 2, 3, 1, 2, 3', etc. in time with the beat.

Listen to some passages of music in triple time. As you listen, tap softly in time with the beat of the music. Choose excerpts from this list:

'Matwala Jiya' from *Mother India*
The theme from *The Young Person's Guide to the Orchestra* by Benjamin Britten
'Danse Macabre' by Saint-Saëns
Violin Concerto in E by Bach (First Movement)
'Das ist ein Floten und Geigen' from *Dichterliebe* by Schumann

COMPOSE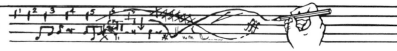

Compose a piece in triple time. You will need an instrument that can play chords.

○ FIRST find different ways of playing chords in triple time. The following suggestions may be useful to start with. Play each one several times, then find three or four more ways.

○ THEN play some of the chord patterns you have discovered on two or three different chords. Try the following:
4 bars of C, then 4 bars of G7
4 bars of C, 2 bars of F, 2 bars of G7
2 bars of C, 2 bars of D minor, 2 bars of F, then 2 bars of C

○ NEXT make a melody to fit the chords. Remember that your melody can consist of just the pitches in the chords, or you can add passing notes if you like.

○ FINALLY practise your music and write it down.

PERFORM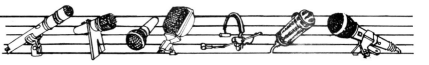

Perform your piece to the rest of your class. As you listen to the others, silently count '1, 2, 3, 1, 2, 3' etc. in time with the beat.

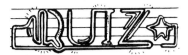

Clarinet Trio by Mozart (Second Movement)

MINUET

1 Which instrument plays the melody at the beginning?

2 Which instrument plays on its own at the end of each section of the minuet?

TRIO – FIRST PLAYING

3 Name the three instruments in the order in which they play in the *trio*.

4 Which of the following patterns represents the rhythm of the viola part?

5 Does the music which links the trio with the minuet contain
a. a drone b. a *sequence* or c. *imitation*?

TRIO – SECOND PLAYING

6 Listen for the following figure, and count the number of times you hear it:
Is it a. 18 times b. 25 times c. 32 times or
d. 42 times?

7 On what sort of scale is this figure based?

THE WHOLE MOVEMENT

8 Describe the difference in character between the minuet and the trio. What musical devices did Mozart use to make this contrast?

RESEARCH

1 Choose *one* of the following topics, and make a report about it for the rest of your class:
   a. Mozart's operas
   b. Mozart's piano music
   c. Mozart's violin music
   d. Mozart's symphonies.
   In your report include a detailed description of *one movement* from your topic.

2 Find out how a 'minuet and trio' form is constructed. To what extent do you think the Second Movement of Mozart's Clarinet Trio is based on this form?

3 Find out about time signatures (see chapter 21 section 3). Then perform three short pieces of music to your class, each with a different time signature. As you listen to the others, try to tell what their time signatures are.

TRY THIS

Piano Concerto No. 21 in C, K467 by Mozart

This is only one of the many popular piano concertos by Mozart. The second movement is the most famous, with its slowly unwinding melody that sounds relaxed but fresh every time it appears. The first movement is a perfect contrast, full of memorable melodies, and imaginative ways of developing them. The last movement is fast and frothy.

Don Giovanni by Mozart (Introduction)

Like almost all operas, *Don Giovanni* has to be seen on stage to be fully appreciated. But it helps if you can get to know some of the music first, and a good starting point is the introduction to *Don Giovanni*. Here there is a short aria, a trio, a few lines of recitative, and a very dramatic story. If you listen to a recording, you might like to follow the words or (better still) a musical score.

16 USING NEW TIMBRES

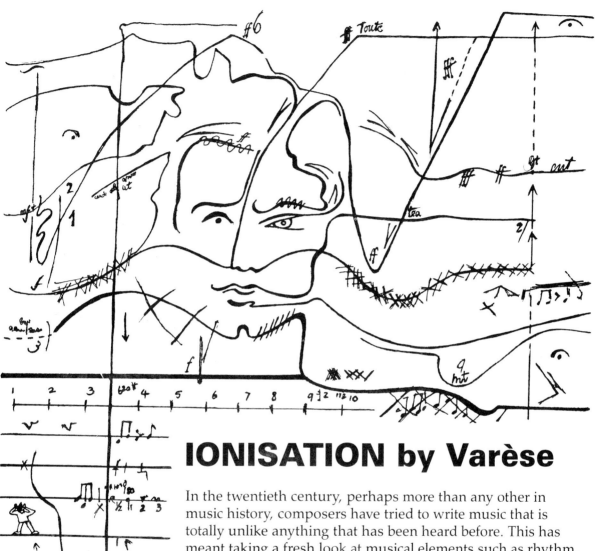

IONISATION by Varèse

In the twentieth century, perhaps more than any other in music history, composers have tried to write music that is totally unlike anything that has been heard before. This has meant taking a fresh look at musical elements such as rhythm, melody and harmony. New and exciting styles have been created with a whole range of new sounds, including electronic colours.

Edgard Varèse loved experimenting with unusual tone colours, and was particularly interested in percussion instruments and electronic music. *Ionisation* is one of his most popular compositions. It is played by thirteen musicians, who play a total of thirty-seven percussion instruments.

START

What would music sound like if there were no melodies at all? Could there be a satisfying piece of music with rhythms instead of melodies?

In New York in the early 1930s, the composer Edgard Varèse asked himself these questions. He came to this conclusion: You can make a good composition without melodies, but you must find different ways of making contrasts.

Varèse decided to use new and unusual timbres. As well as the usual percussion instruments – bass drums, snare drums, cymbals and tambourines – he used these instruments:

sirens
cow bells
a 'lion roar' effect
a slap stick
sleigh bells

He also used an assortment of folk instruments such as Jamaican bongos and Cuban claves, and he used melodic instruments such as a piano to make thick, quiet chords instead of melodies.

COMPOSE

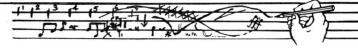

Compose a piece without melodies. As well as the normal percussion instruments you will need a wide range of new tone colours and vocal sounds. (You might like to create the effect of sirens.) Here are some you might use: twanging rulers, plastic cartons filled and shaken, metal tins tapped on the bottom or side, mugs hanging from their handles, metal zips, etc. Make a large collection before you start.

○ FIRST start to make a graphic score. Write your instruments down the left of your page, and either bars, or time (in seconds) along the top.

For example:

Time (seconds)	0	5	10	15	20	25	30
Ruler							
Wooden sticks							
Small tins							
Medium tins							
Large tins							
Snare drum							

○ THEN see how many different ways you can find of making
interesting tone colours with your instruments. For each
method of playing, write down a symbol. For example:

shake
scrape (with metal)
scrape (with wood)
tap (with metal)
tap (with wood)
roll, etc.

Find ways of making four or five different tone colours from
each instrument, choosing those that make the greatest
contrast.

○ NEXT start your composition, using some of these ingredients:

contrasts of tense, quiet sections with loud and forceful
sections
sudden interruptions
contrasts of metal, wood, plastic and vocal tone colours
contrasts of thin and thick textures
some sections which sound urgent
some sections which might remind you of rush-hour cities.

As you decide on the sounds you want, write them in your
graphic score. Use pencil so that you can change your mind if
you discover better effects, and remember to include dynamic
markings in your score.

○ FINALLY when your score is complete ask some friends to
help you to perform it. While you are rehearsing your music
try to make sure that every sound is played as you wish, but
do not be afraid of changing your music as you hear it.

93

PERFORM

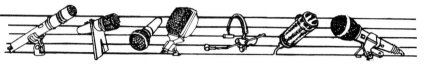

Perform your music to the rest of your class. As you listen to the others try to hear how each piece uses contrasts.

Ionisation by Varèse

THE FIRST THIRD (0–2 MINUTES APPROX.) PLAYED 4 TIMES

1 Does the music start *p*, *mp*, *f* or *ff*?

2 How many sirens do you hear?

3 Play this rhythm:

Rhythm A

What instrument plays it?

4 Write the rhythm, and insert a ***sforzando*** sign (*sf*) over the loudest note.

5 In the quiet sounds that follow rhythm A, do you hear

    a. mainly metal instruments
    b. mainly wooden instruments
    c. mainly drums?

6 When rhythm A is repeated twice, shortly afterwards, is it

    a. shorter
    b. longer
    c. the same length as the first time?

THE SECOND THIRD (2–4 MINUTES APPROX.) PLAYED 4 TIMES

7 For several bars, there are no sirens. Then, when one does start to play, it is accompanied by six separate rhythms. Name two of the instruments that play those rhythms.

8 Immediately afterwards, you will hear several instruments playing the following rhythm:

Rhythm B

Suggest a suitable dynamic marking for it.

9   Are the rhythms which follow rhythm B

a. faster
b. slower
c. the same speed as rhythm B?

10   When the siren plays again, is it accompanied by

a. mainly metal instruments
b. mainly wooden instruments
c. mainly drums?

**THE FINAL THIRD (4–6 MINUTES APPROX.) PLAYED
4 TIMES**

11   After this rhythm finishes, you will hear a crash on metal
instruments and siren, with a pause. Then you will hear bass
drums. Which of these rhythms do they play?

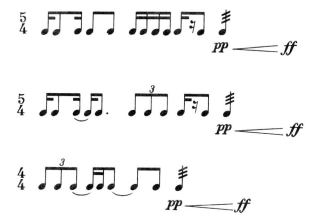

12   How many times do you hear that rhythm?

13   Shortly afterwards there is one bar marked *pp*. Which
instrument plays a very fast, light rhythm in this bar?

14   When the piano and tubular bells enter, does the music

a. get slower
b. get faster
c. remain at the same speed?

15   Describe some of the contrasts that you hear in *Ionisation*.

RESEARCH

1   Imagine that you have just attended the first-ever performance of *Ionisation*. Make a report about it for a friend who has never heard anything like it. Describe the music in detail, and explain how you might have felt about being at the first performance of this 'unusual' piece of music.

2   Find out about electronic music. Choose one of the following topics, and make a short report about it for the rest of your class. Also try to listen to at least one recording which includes your choice:

musique concrète
synthesisers   sequencers
feedback   samplers
electric drum-machines digital delay

3   Find out about the following instruments that Varèse uses in *Ionisation*: anvils, cow bell, snare drum, tom-tom. Name and describe or draw any five other percussion instruments.

TRY THIS

Poème Electronique by Varèse

TAPE
This is an early and very exciting piece of electronic music. It is quite long (about 25 minutes) but the contrasts and colours are so vivid it is worth getting to know section by section. (You need good equipment to appreciate it properly!)

'Lux Aeterna' by Ligeti

CHOIR
The English title of this piece is 'Eternal Light', meaning 'the light of heaven'. What would music be like without any rhythm? It is an impossible question, of course, but Ligeti comes as close as anyone to answering it. This short vocal piece is almost entirely concerned with colours, pitches and textures, and conjures up a picture of the quiet, intense light of the title.

17 PROGRAMME MUSIC

'DANSE MACABRE'
by Saint-Saëns

The idea of telling a story through music has been around for many years, but at the end of the nineteenth century it became very popular. Many composers used stories or poems to inspire their compositions, and music which reflected these became known as **programme** music.

One of the most famous of these composers was the French musician, Camille Saint-Saëns. He wrote several pieces of programme music, and the reason that his music is still so popular today is probably that it is well designed and melodic, and it does not just 'tell a story'. 'Danse Macabre' is one of Saint-Saëns' most popular works. It has an exciting programme, and is also a good example of how Saint-Saëns could develop his musical ideas.

START

When you listen to songs, do you concentrate on the music? Or do you think mostly about the words?

Although much of the music you hear probably has words, a great deal has no words, and must be understood in purely musical terms. In other words, you understand the music by listening for the contrasts and repetitions, the tensions and relaxations, the rhythmic drive and so on.

A third type of music has an extra idea connected with it. This can be a theme (*The Four Seasons* by Vivaldi) or a story (*Romeo and Juliet* by Tchaikovsky) or even paintings (*Pictures at an Exhibition* by Mussorgsky) This sort of music is called programme music.

One famous piece of programme music is called 'Danse Macabre', and is based on a poem of the same name.
The original poem, 'Danse Macabre', is in French, but here it is for you to read in an English translation. Read it several times in different ways, and try to bring out the weird and spooky atmosphere by the way you read it.

Zig-a-zig-a-zig – it's the rhythm of Death!
His heels tap the tombstones as he tunes his violin.
Death at midnight, playing a dance-tune –
Zig-a-zig-a-zig on his violin.
The winter wind whistles and the night is dark;
The winter wind whistles and the lime-trees moan.
Weird, white skeletons streak across the shadows;
Running and leaping, wrapped in their shrouds.
Zig-a-zig-a-zig – the dance grows even wilder;
You can hear the eerie clatter of the dancer's bones . . .
But wait! Suddenly, they all stop dancing!
They scatter . . . they vanish – for the cock has crowed.

'Danse Macabre' by Henri Cazalis

COMPOSE

Compose a piece of programme music based on 'Danse Macabre'. You can use whatever instruments are available, and you may decide to use unusual tone colours such as those you used in chapter 16. You can use a graphic score to write down your music.

○ FIRST read the poem once more to decide what its mood and atmosphere are. Then choose some of the images in the poem, and decide what sort of music would suit them best. Choose from these lists:

Some elements of the poem

The chimes of midnight
Death's heels on the tombstones
Death's violin
the winter wind
the clatter of the skeletons' bones
the dance growing wilder
the cock-crow
Death and the skeletons vanishing

For example, Death's violin might be represented by a violin melody played on **open strings**; the skeletons' bones might be represented by xylophone **tremolandos**, etc.

○ NEXT put your ideas together to make your music. The overall *form* of your composition should reflect that of the poem:

Death appears – the dance starts – gets wilder – stops – everyone vanishes.

Remember you can use musical devices such as ostinatos, drones, arpeggios, sequences, etc. to help build your music. Try to include many variations on your musical ideas.

○ FINALLY practise your music and write it down, using a graphic score if necessary. If you need help performing your music, ask your teacher or some friends.

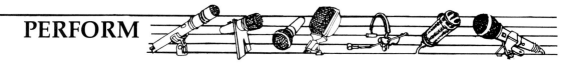

PERFORM

Perform your music to the rest of your class. As you listen to the others, try to hear how each piece uses musical elements to describe the atmosphere of 'Danse Macabre'.

LISTEN

Listen to 'Danse Macabre' by Saint-Saëns. How many of the poem's details are depicted in the music?

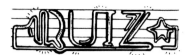

'Danse Macabre' by Saint-Saëns

These questions will involve you in a long analysis of
'Danse Macabre'. At the end of it you will have greatly
increased your knowledge of how music can be constructed.

Here are the main themes from 'Danse Macabre'. Choose one,
and play it for the rest of your class.

FIRST SECTION (BARS 1–137)

1 Which theme contains a passage based on the chromatic scale?

2 Which theme is played in fifths?

3 Which theme do you hear first and which instrument plays it?

4 Which theme do you hear second and which instrument plays it?

5 Which theme do you hear third and which instrument plays it?

6 Listen to this music. On which theme is it based?

7 Listen to this music. On which theme is it based?

8 Listen to the repeat of themes D and A. What differences are there between the first time you hear them and the second?

SECOND SECTION (BARS 138–197)

9 On which theme is the fugue-like section based?

10 You will hear theme B played twice. Name two differences between the two playings.

11 Theme B is a parody of the following melody from the Roman Catholic Mass for the Dead (Requiem). Explain briefly how Saint-Saëns parodies the Requiem melody.

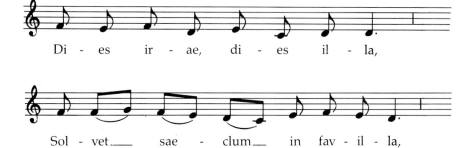

THIRD SECTION (BARS 198–262)

12 Listen to this music, then write down

    a. which instruments play it
    b. on which theme it is based
    c. how it develops the theme.

13　How many times do you hear theme F in the following section?

14　Listen to theme A, played in stretto by **brass** instruments. Can you guess what 'stretto' means?

15　Listen to the following music, played by cellos and basses. On which theme is it based?

FOURTH SECTION (BARS 263–355)

16　Listen to the following music, played by **woodwind** and brass. What is the relationship between the melody (top **line**) and the bass (bottom **line**)?

17　Listen carefully to the strings playing part of the same music immediately afterwards. What differences are there between the woodwind's and the strings' versions?

18 Which theme accompanies the following music?

FIFTH SECTION (BARS 356–428)

19 At the climax of 'Danse Macabre', which two themes are played at the same time?

20 Listen to the following music, played by violins. On what sort of scale is it based?

21 Listen to the following music, played by the whole orchestra. On what theme is it based?

SIXTH SECTION (BARS 429 TO END)

22   Which instrument plays theme E?

23   Listen to the final bars of 'Danse Macabre' (below). How is theme E developed in these nine bars?

24   What sort of cadence is played in the last two bars?

THE WHOLE OF 'DANSE MACABRE' PLAYED ONCE

25   Make a list of all the elements of the poem which you think you can hear. Say how they are depicted in the music.

RESEARCH

1 Write a record-sleeve note for 'Danse Macabre', emphasising the atmosphere that the music creates. Make people want to listen to it!

2 Listen to one of the following pieces of programme music, and discover how the 'programme' of each is reflected in the music:

Symphonie Fantastique by Berlioz
'Les Préludes' by Liszt
Romeo and Juliet by Tchaikovsky
The *Hebrides* Overture by Mendelssohn

3 Analyse one short piece of music you know to discover
a. which are the main themes   b. how these are developed
c. what is the form of the music.
Choose from this list:

'Matwala Jiya' from *Mother India*
Syrinx by Debussy
Symphony No. 9 'From the New World' by Dvořák (Second Movement)

TRY THIS

Carnival of the Animals by Saint-Saëns
CHAMBER ORCHESTRA AND PIANO DUET
This is a set of fourteen short pieces, depicting members of the animal kingdom, including pianists practising their scales. The most famous – a beautifully still cello solo – is 'The Swan'. All the pieces are worth listening to, particularly 'Fossils' and 'Finale'.

The Organ Symphony by Saint-Saëns
ORCHESTRA, PIANO DUET AND ORGAN
Saint-Saëns is generally thought of as a stylish and witty but essentially frivolous composer, who could produce tuneful little pieces, but not much else. However, his Organ Symphony is a thoroughly satisfying full-scale composition, still tuneful, but with genuinely powerful and moving moments. Make time to listen to the whole symphony or, if possible, attend a live performance.

18 USING THREE CHORDS

'WEST END BLUES'
performed by
Louis Armstrong
and his Hot Five

For many popular musicians, the style that started it all was the *blues*. An enormous amount of rock music and jazz has its roots in this one style, which was born some time near the beginning of the twentieth century, largely in the bars, brothels and nightclubs of the American South.

Most blues songs have a deep sadness in them, and many are about the feelings you have when your loved one leaves you. Despite this, many completely different songs have been composed in blues style.

Play this chord progression:

Note: these chords are not easy for guitar, so guitarists may prefer to tune their strings down a semitone and play chords of E, A and B⁷.

This progression is very popular, particularly in early blues songs. In fact, it is so popular that it has its own name. It is called 'twelve bar blues', or sometimes 'twelve bar' or 'blues form' for short.

Twelve bar blues

‖:	I	I	I	I⁷	IV	IV	I	I	V⁷	IV	I	V⁷ :‖
	1	2	3	4	5	6	7	8	9	10	11	12

(For an explanation of these chord symbols, see chapter 21 section 8.)

Many songs have been composed to fit the twelve bar blues, and often these songs take the form of a call and response. The call is usually sung, and the response played by a melodic instrument.

PERFORM

Perform 'West End Blues'. The melody (below) should be sung wherever there are words, and one instrument should improvise each response. Other instruments can play the chords, or make up a quiet repeated drum rhythm based on this pattern:

'West End Blues' Words and music by Joe Oliver and Clarence Williams

This song uses the chords of the twelve bar blues.

When you have performed the song as written, perform it again, taking it in turns to improvise new responses. Play through the song about ten times, trying as many different responses as you can.

COMPOSE

Soon after the twelve bar chord progression was born, some blues musicians became dissatisfied with simply repeating the melody many times. So, often, the singer or an instrumentalist performed the melody more or less as it had been written; and then members of the band took turns at improvising solos. At the end of the song the singer sang the melody again. Both the song melody and the improvised solos often used the twelve bar blues, and each playing of this chord progression was called a chorus.

Compose a chorus to go with 'West End Blues'.

○ FIRST be sure that you know the chords in the twelve bar blues. If possible you should be able to listen to the chords while you compose your chorus. You can do this in several ways:

a. Play the chords with your left hand on a keyboard instrument. (This is the best way, and well worth the effort.)
b. Record the chords on tape.
c. Programme the chords into a keyboard (not all keyboards have this facility).
d. Ask your teacher or a friend to play the chords.

○ NEXT play two or three melodic figures from 'West End Blues'. Play them several times to fix them in your mind, then use them at different pitch levels to fit with the chords of the twelve bar blues. Do this four bars at a time, using mainly the notes of the chords. Include 'extra' notes and blue notes if you can.

○ FINALLY practise your chorus until you can perform it without hesitations. Then write it down so that you do not forget it. If you have time, try to compose another chorus, different from the first.

Perform your chorus(es) with the rest of your class. Perform the melody of 'West End Blues' first, then take turns to play the choruses you have composed. Finally play the melody again. Does this remind you of any form in Classical music?

LISTEN

Listen to 'West End Blues' performed by Louis Armstrong and his Hot Five. Which choruses stick exactly to the chords of the twelve bar blues?

Listen again, and play along quietly with the chords (p. 108).

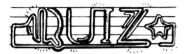

'West End Blues' performed by Louis Armstrong and his Hot Five

FIRST PLAYING
1 Name all the instruments you hear.

SECOND PLAYING
2 Name the solos in the order in which you hear them.

THIRD PLAYING (INTRODUCTION AND FIRST CHORUS)
3 Which of these graphic shapes best fits the solo in the introduction?

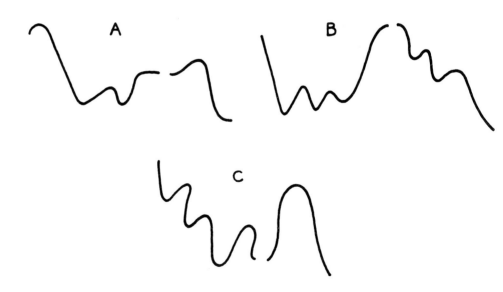

4 What do you hear between the unaccompanied solo at the beginning, and the first chorus?

5 In the first chorus, does the piano play a. melody
b. counter-melody   c. chords or   d. ostinato?

FOURTH PLAYING

6   In the second chorus, what is the difference between the music of the left hand and that of the right hand?

7   Describe the vocal music in the third chorus.

FIFTH PLAYING (FOURTH AND FIFTH CHORUSES)

8   What instruments accompany the piano in the fourth chorus?

9   Listen to the fifth chorus, then write out the first four bars of the trumpet and clarinet parts. The first two notes of the trumpet part have been done for you.

SIXTH PLAYING (THE WHOLE PIECE)

10   What ornament does the trumpet play on the very last note?

RESEARCH

1   Listen to two songs from *20 Greatest Hits Vol. One* by Elvis Presley. Listen carefully, and try to decide which chords you hear, and in which order. Check your answer by playing the chords along with the recording.
Choose from this list:
'Blue Suede Shoes'
'Hound Dog'
'All Shook Up'
'Teddy Bear'
'I Got Stung'

2   Find out what chords I, IV and V are in the following keys:

Bb F C G D major

G D A E B minor

Write them down as arpeggios and as block chords.
(See chapter 21 section 7.)
Choose any two songs, and play them in one of these keys. As you play them, harmonise them using chords I, IV and V. (This will only work if all the notes of the melody are notes of the scale.)

3   Choose one of the following blues musicians, and make a
    report about him or her for the rest of your class. Include a
    description of at least two of their songs: Muddy Waters,
    Robert Johnson, Howlin' Wolf, Bessie Smith, Billie Holiday.

TRY THIS

The World's Greatest Blues Singer
by Bessie Smith

This is the title of a double LP by the woman who is generally
recognised as one of the greatest blues singers of all time. She
has a beautifully rich and powerful voice but her tone is made
apparently without any effort. A few of her songs such as
'Hustlin' Dan' and 'Black Mountain Blues' are based on the
twelve bar blues, and if you listen carefully you can play along
with the chords.

'Since I've Been Loving You'
by Led Zeppelin

This song, from the album *Led Zeppelin 3*, is an example of how
much variety the blues could have. It uses the twelve bar blues
progression, and contains a good deal of the blues spirit, but
otherwise is totally different from anything by either Bessie
Smith or Louis Armstrong. The overall effect of vast space is
created partly by an extremely slow tempo – each twelve-bar
chorus lasts for well over a minute.

19 RONDO FORM

VIOLIN CONCERTO IN E
by Bach

Although millions of people today think of Bach as the greatest composer ever, when he was alive he was admired mainly as an organist. His compositions were thought old-fashioned and second-rate, and very few of them were printed. One reason was perhaps that Bach *was* old-fashioned. He preferred to compose in the *Baroque* style, while others preferred the simpler and more immediately tuneful Classical style. Also, Bach did not act like a 'star'. He lived quietly, worked incredibly hard, and did not travel. He wrote his music for practical purposes, for his church choir or for his small court orchestra.

Many years after he died, however, musicians began to recognise his genius, through the discovery of such great masterpieces as the *St Matthew Passion* and the B minor Mass.

START

Play this melody:

How many times do you play the following figures or similar ones?

A

B

How has Bach used the figures to construct his melody?

LISTEN

You have probably discovered that most of the melody is based on the music of the first two bars. Now listen to the whole of the last movement of Bach's Violin Concerto in E. How many times do you hear the melody you have played? What else do you hear?

You probably noticed that the melody you played is repeated several times, with other music between the repeats. This makes a satisfying and simple musical form called *rondo* form.

RONDO FORM

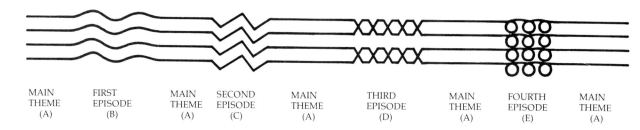

MAIN THEME (A)	FIRST EPISODE (B)	MAIN THEME (A)	SECOND EPISODE (C)	MAIN THEME (A)	THIRD EPISODE (D)	MAIN THEME (A)	FOURTH EPISODE (E)	MAIN THEME (A)

Now listen again to the third movement of Bach's Violin Concerto in E, following the form of the music with the diagram above.

COMPOSE

Compose a piece in rondo form. You can use whatever instruments are available.

○ FIRST construct your main theme. Ideally this should be the most interesting section, but keep it fairly short (six to eight bars will do), as it will be heard several times. This theme can be a rhythmic phrase, a melody, a series of chords, or a melody with chords.
It can involve drones, ostinatos, sequences, or melodies in thirds, fourths, or other intervals. If you decide to make a melody, you may use one of the forms you met before, or you might like to base your own melody on that by Bach. Write down your main theme.

○ NEXT construct two or three episodes. It is a good idea to have at least one episode that is in a different key, as this will provide variety. As you finish each episode write it down.

If you find it difficult to begin an episode try this:

a. Take a few notes from your main theme.
b. Change them in some way.
c. Use them to make the beginning of your episode.

For example, if you take the first bar of Bach's main theme:

turn it upside-down, beginning on B:

add one note:

and put the last three notes an octave higher:

you will have the first bar of the first episode!

○ FINALLY practise your music. As you do so, listen to the contrast made by the main theme and the episodes. How can these be brought out by your performance?

 **PERFORM**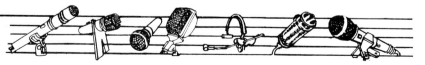

Perform your rondo to the rest of your class. As you listen to others, try to identify the main theme and the episodes.

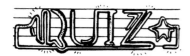

Violin Concerto in E by Bach
(Third Movement)

THEME AND FIRST TWO EPISODES

1 What instruments do you hear?

2 Suggest a suitable word to describe the tempo of the music.

3 Are the episodes played   a. louder   b. softer   c. at the same dynamic level as the main theme?

4 In the first episode, are there   a. more   b. less or   c. the same number of instruments as in the theme?

5 Is the first episode in a major or minor key?

6 Is the second episode in a major or minor key?

THEME AND SECOND TWO EPISODES

7 Which of the following extracts is the bass line at the start of the third episode?

A

B

C

8 Compare the first two phrases of the fourth episode. Is the second phrase

   a. a repeat of the first
   b. a tone lower than the first
   c. a tone higher than the first
   d. a third higher than the first?

THE WHOLE MOVEMENT

9 In which episode does the soloist perform **double stopping**?

10 What contrasts of expression are there in this music?

RESEARCH

1 Learn about oratorio, and write down the meanings of the following: recitatives, arias, **duets**, choruses, **chorales**. Find out the names of five oratorios, two by Bach and three by other composers. Finally, listen to the first part of Bach's *St Matthew Passion*, and see if you can recognise the recitatives, arias, etc.

2 Find out about **polyphony**. What is the difference between music which is mainly polyphonic, that which is mainly **monophonic** and that which is mainly **homophonic**? Which sort did Bach chiefly compose?

3 Each of the following pieces of music is in rondo form. Listen to one of them, and see if you can recognise the main theme and the episodes:

a. 'Für Elise' by Beethoven
b. Prelude to *Carmen* by Bizet
c. 'Pavane pour une Infante Defunte' by Ravel

4 Find out about how orchestras changed from one period of music history to the next. What were the main differences between Baroque, Classical and Romantic orchestras? Listen to these examples:

Violin Concerto in E by Bach (Baroque)
'The Surprise' Symphony by Haydn (Classical)
Symphony No. 9 'From the New World' by Dvořák (Romantic)

Orchestral Suite No. 3 by Bach

ORCHESTRA

In Bach's time, a **suite** was a set of dances. One of the most popular of Baroque suites is the Orchestral Suite No. 3 by Bach. After a long and complex **overture**, there is a slow relaxed air, and then three lively dances, a **gavotte**, a **bourrée** and a jig. Listen for the famous violin solo in the air, and for the brilliant high trumpet playing in the later movements.

The *Messiah* by Handel

SOLO SINGERS, CHORUS AND ORCHESTRA

Handel was one of the other great composers of the Baroque times. He spent much of his working life in England and, perhaps for that reason, his music has always been especially popular in the United Kingdom.

The *Messiah* is an oratorio, with words from different parts of the Bible. It is traditionally performed at around Christmas time, by choirs all over Britain.

Try to attend a live performance by a good choir, and before you go, get to know some of the most famous pieces. Some of these are arias, such as 'I Know That My Redeemer Liveth' and 'The Trumpet Shall Sound'. Others are choruses such as 'Worthy is the Lamb' and the famous 'Hallelujah Chorus'.

20 MORE ACCOMPANIMENT PATTERNS

DICHTERLIEBE
by Schumann

Robert Schumann wrote music in the Romantic style which was popular throughout the nineteenth century. His music always had a deeply personal emotional meaning, and much of it was written for the great love of his life, Clara, whom he eventually married – much against the wishes of her father.

Clara was a fine composer herself, and also an internationally famous pianist, so she played the first performances of many of her husband's pieces. With their glorious, singing melodies, and their characteristic chromatic harmonies, many of them were immediately popular. Robert Schumann is still one of music's best-loved composers.

START

Choose one of the following musical examples, and play it for the rest of your class. Listen to all of them. What do you notice?

You probably heard that each was based on the same sequence of chords. In fact, each example displays a different way of playing exactly the same chord sequence:

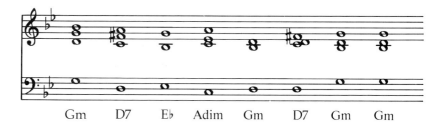

| Gm | D7 | Eb | Adim | Gm | D7 | Gm | Gm |

Can you find three or four additional ways of playing the same sequence of chords?

Perform your examples to the rest of your class. As you listen to the others, count how many different ways your class has discovered.

LISTEN

Schumann uses different ways of playing chords in his **song cycle** *Dichterliebe* ('Dichterliebe' is German for 'poet's love'). In some of the songs, the pianist accompanies the singer with chords, using different accompaniment patterns. Listen to the following songs from *Dichterliebe*:

No. 3 'Die Rose, die Lilie'
No. 7 'Ich Grolle Nicht'
No. 9 'Das ist ein Floten und Geigen'
No. 10 'Hör ich das Liedchen Klingen'

Which song uses which accompaniment pattern (A, B, C or D)?

Which song uses the sequence of chords above?

COMPOSE
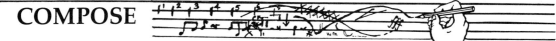

Compose a piece of music using some of the accompaniment patterns you have discovered. You will need two friends who play different melodic instruments to perform the finished version.

○ FIRST make a melody in ternary form. You may like to use one from a previous chapter. Then find out which are the main chords for the key (see chapter 21 section 7).

○ NEXT choose the chords to fit your melody, and harmonise one phrase at a time. Generally you will need one chord or maybe two chords to each bar. Remember that some of the melody notes may be 'extra' notes but that most of them will probably be chord notes. As you fit the chords to your melody listen very carefully to be sure that they fit well.

○ THEN decide on three accompaniment patterns for your melody, one for each section. Also decide on two different melodic instruments. Practise playing the accompaniment patterns yourself, using the chords you have discovered, and teach the melody to your two friends.

○ FINALLY organise your piece like this:

SECTION A	*SECTION B*	*SECTION A*
First accompaniment pattern	Second accompaniment pattern	Third accompaniment pattern
Instrument 1	Instrument 2	Instruments 1 and 2

Practise it and write it down.

PERFORM

Perform your music to the rest of your class. As you listen to the others, decide how you would write the rhythm of their accompaniment patterns.

LISTEN

Listen to 'Ich Grolle Nicht' and follow the music on pp. 125–27. Then answer the questions on p. 128.

'Ich Grolle Nicht' by Schumann

strahlst in Di - a - man-tenpracht, es fällt kein Strahl in dei -nes

Herzens Nacht. Das weiss ich längst. _____

Ich grolle nicht und wenn das Herz _____ auch

bricht. Ich sah dich ja im Trau - me, und sah die

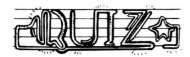 'Ich Grolle Nicht' from *Dichterliebe* by Schumann

1 In what key is this song?

2 What does the sign > mean, and what effect does it have on the music?

3 Listen carefully to the note that is sung on the word 'Herz' (bar 3), and write the **accidental** that should appear before the note.

4 Why do you think the composer wanted the three notes in the left hand of the piano part in bars 12–14 to sound loud?

5 What is the meaning of the word '*ritard.*' in bars 16 and 28?

6 In which bar does the second verse begin?

7 In the version you are hearing, does the soloist sing the lower or the upper notes in bars 27–29?

8 How many different chords are there in the last five bars?

9 Name *two* places where you hear a sequence.

10 Schumann wrote only six dynamic markings in the vocal part (*mf*, *f*, *f*, *p*, *cresc*, *f*). Listen carefully to your recording, and write if, and where, you think the soloist deviates from these markings.

11 What sort of cadence is played in the last two bars?

12 Describe how the mood in this song changes from the beginning to the end.

RESEARCH

1 Find a song which has a melody with chord symbols printed above the stave. Play the melody with the chords, using an accompaniment pattern that fits well.

2 The following composers lived at the same time as Schumann. Listen to, and make a report about one piece of music by any one of them: Berlioz, Mendelssohn, Brahms, Chopin, Liszt, Wagner.

3 Choose three pieces of music from the following list, and listen to the accompaniments to the melodies. How do their accompaniment patterns change during the music?

'The Wife of the Soldier'   by Martin Carthy
'The Boxer'   by Simon and Garfunkel
Violin Concerto in E   by Bach
'War'   by Bob Marley and the Wailers
The Young Person's Guide
to the Orchestra   by Britten

TRY THIS

Piano Concerto in A Minor by Schumann

PIANO AND ORCHESTRA

This is an enormously popular Romantic piece. The music has many stirringly heroic moments, although the general atmosphere is one of lyrical, calm beauty. The first and third movements contain some exciting and demanding music for the pianist, as well as many lush melodies for orchestra. The second movement is less dramatic, but is tender, and quite fast.

Album for the Young by Schumann

PIANO

This collection contains some of the most popular of all easy piano music. Some of the pieces – 'Melody' and 'Soldiers' March' – are of around grade 1 standard, while others such as 'Mignon' and 'Remembrance' are typical of Schumann at his best. There are several lively pieces, but most of the best music has a touching and wistful character.

21 USEFUL THEORY

1 NOTE VALUES AND RESTS

SHAPE	NAME	REST	RELATIVE LENGTH
o	semibreve	▬	4 beats
♩.	dotted minim	▬·	3 beats
♩	minim	▬	2 beats
♩.	dotted crotchet	૪· or ૪·	1½ beats
♩	crotchet	૪ or ૪	1 beat
♪	quaver	૪	½ beat
♪	semiquaver	૪	¼ beat
♪	demisemiquaver	૪	⅛ beat

Where two or more quavers, semiquavers or demisemiquavers are played together, they are usually written like this:

♫ quavers

♬ semiquavers

♬ demisemiquavers

2 PITCH

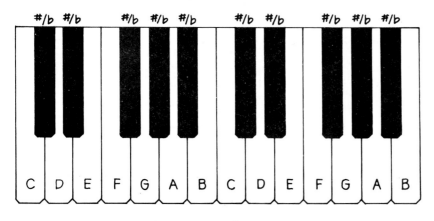

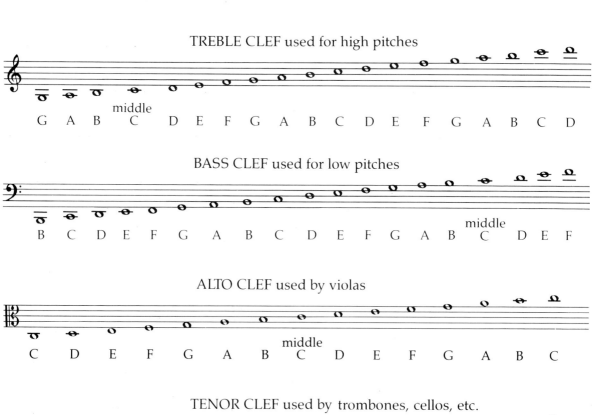

TREBLE CLEF used for high pitches

G A B middle C D E F G A B C D E F G A B C D

BASS CLEF used for low pitches

B C D E F G A B C D E F G A B middle C D E F

ALTO CLEF used by violas

C D E F G A B middle C D E F G A B C

TENOR CLEF used by trombones, cellos, etc.

A B C D E F G A B middle C D E F G A

ACCIDENTALS

A sharp sign (♯) before a note makes that note a semitone higher.

A flat sign (♭) before a note makes that note a semitone lower.

A natural sign (♮) before a note puts that note back to normal. (For examples of accidentals, see p. 143.)

3 TIME SIGNATURES

TIME SIGNATURE	MEANING	MAIN BEATS
$\frac{2}{2}$	Two minim beats in each bar	
$\frac{2}{4}$	Two crotchet beats in each bar	
$\frac{3}{4}$	Three crotchet beats in each bar	
$\frac{4}{4}$ or **C**	Four crotchet beats in each bar	
$\frac{6}{4}$	Six crotchet beats* in each bar	
$\frac{3}{8}$	Three quaver beats in each bar	
$\frac{6}{8}$	Six quaver beats** in each bar	
$\frac{9}{8}$	Nine quaver beats** in each bar	
$\frac{12}{8}$	Twelve quaver beats** in each bar	

* The main beat in this time signature is the dotted minim beat.

** The main beat in these time signatures is the dotted crotchet beat.

With the other time signatures in this table, three equal notes are occasionally played in the time of two. These are called triplets and usually look either like this: or this:

4 GROUPS OF NOTES

Where two or more quavers or shorter notes come together, they should be joined together in groups and the notes should be grouped so that each group fills one beat. For example:

BEAT   1   2   3   4   1   2   3   4

5 INTERVALS

An interval is the distance between two notes, whether they are played together or one after the other.

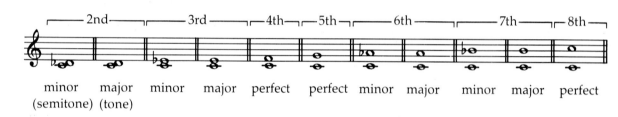

minor   major   minor   major   perfect   perfect   minor   major   minor   major   perfect
(semitone) (tone)

An interval which is a semitone *more* than a major or perfect interval is called 'augmented'.

An interval which is a semitone *less* than a perfect or minor interval is called 'diminished'.
For example:

augmented 4th   diminished 4th

6 SCALES

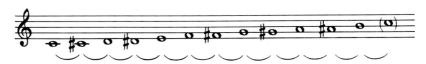

CHROMATIC SCALE all the intervals are semitones

WHOLE TONE SCALE all the intervals are tones

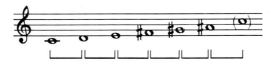

In major and minor scales, each degree has a name:

Tonic Supertonic Mediant Subdominant Dominant Submediant Leading-note

For example:

SCALE OF C MAJOR

NATURAL SCALE OF C MINOR (ALSO CALLED AEOLIAN MODE)

HARMONIC SCALE OF C MINOR

MELODIC SCALE OF C MINOR

Tonic   Supertonic   Mediant   Subdominant   Dominant   Submediant   Leading-note   Tonic

The descending scale is the same as the natural minor scale. Whichever minor scale is used, the key signature is always that of the natural minor scale (see next section).

7 KEYS

The following shows the key signatures and main chords for all the common major and minor keys.

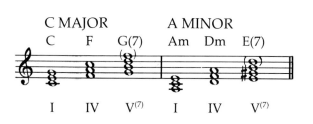

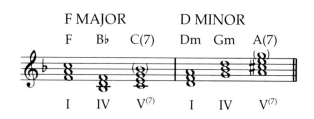

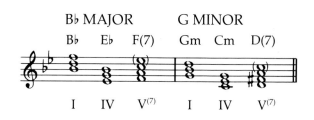

A MAJOR   F# MINOR
A   D   E(7)   F#m Bm C#(7)

I   IV   V(7)   I   IV   V(7)

E♭ MAJOR   C MINOR
E♭ A♭ B♭(7)   Cm Fm G(7)

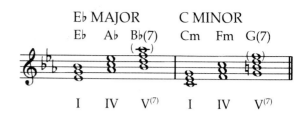

I   IV   V(7)   I   IV   V(7)

E MAJOR   C# MINOR
E   A   B(7)   C#m F#m G#(7)

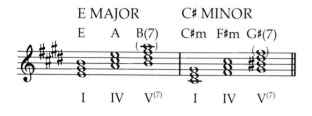

I   IV   V(7)   I   IV   V(7)

A♭ MAJOR   F MINOR
A♭ D♭ E♭(7)   Fm B♭m C(7)

I   IV   V(7)   I   IV   V(7)

B MAJOR   G# MINOR
B   E   F#(7)   G#m C#m D#(7)

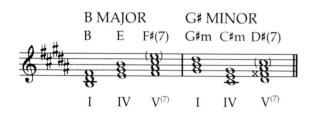

I   IV   V(7)   I   IV   V(7)

D♭ MAJOR   B♭ MINOR
D♭ G♭ A♭(7)   B♭m E♭m F(7)

I   IV   V(7)   I   IV   V(7)

F# MAJOR   D# MINOR
F# B C#(7)   D#m G#m A#(7)

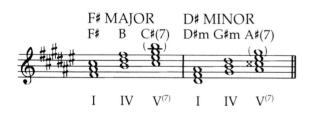

I   IV   V(7)   I   IV   V(7)

G♭ MAJOR   E♭ MINOR
G♭ C♭ D♭(7)   E♭m A♭m B♭(7)

I   IV   V(7)   I   IV   V(7)

8 COMMON CHORDS

Common chords contain the root (the note on which the chord is based), as well as two other notes, a third above the root, and a fifth above the root. Therefore a chord of C major contains C (the root), E (the major third), and G (the fifth):

A chord of C minor contains C (the root), E♭ (the minor 3rd), and G (the fifth):

Chords can be built on all degrees of a scale. Sometimes they are called by the name of that degree (tonic, supertonic, mediant, etc.). Sometimes they are called by number, and written down as Roman numerals (I, II, III, etc.). Sometimes they are called by the name of the root (A, B, C, etc.).

CHORDS IN C MAJOR

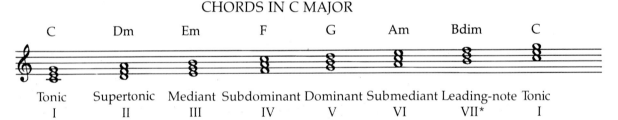

C	Dm	Em	F	G	Am	Bdim	C
Tonic	Supertonic	Mediant	Subdominant	Dominant	Submediant	Leading-note	Tonic
I	II	III	IV	V	VI	VII*	I

* rarely used

CHORDS IN C MINOR

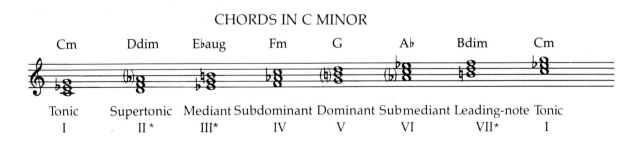

Cm	Ddim	E♭aug	Fm	G	A♭	Bdim	Cm
Tonic	Supertonic	Mediant	Subdominant	Dominant	Submediant	Leading-note	Tonic
I	II *	III*	IV	V	VI	VII*	I

* rarely used

When the root is the bottom note, the chord is in ROOT POSITION:

When the 3rd is the bottom note, the chord is in FIRST INVERSION:

When the 5th is the bottom note, the chord is in SECOND INVERSION:

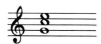

9 CADENCES

A cadence is a progression of chords which is played at the end of phrases in quite a lot of tonal music.

Common cadences include:

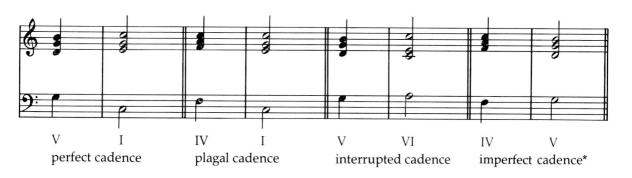

V	I	IV	I	V	VI	IV	V
perfect cadence		plagal cadence		interrupted cadence		imperfect cadence*	

*Imperfect cadences can be formed by various chords followed by the dominant. Chords I/V, IV/V and IIb/V are the most common.

PERFECT and PLAGAL cadences have the same effect as a musical full stop, and are used to make a phrase sound finished. IMPERFECT and INTERRUPTED cadences have the same effect as a musical comma, and are used to make the music sound as if it must continue.

10 DOMINANT 7TH CHORDS

7th chords are similar to common chords, but contain an extra note, the seventh above the root. The most common 7th chord is the dominant 7th (V^7), and it is usually followed by the chord of I or VI.

In the key of C major, the dominant 7th chord is:

The 7th almost always falls when the next chord comes. For example:

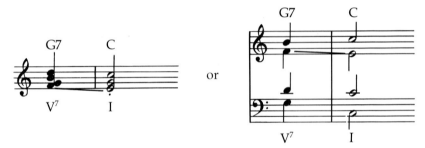

or

OTHER ADDED NOTE CHORDS

These include:

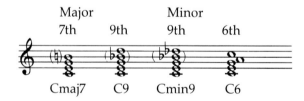

They can be formed on any degree of the scale and, used musically, can have a variety of effects on your harmonies.

11 MELODIC DEVELOPMENT

You can develop a melody or melodic figure in many ways.
These are a few of the most common.

You can repeat a figure at a higher or lower pitch:

SEQUENCE: Violin Concerto in E by Bach

You can repeat a figure in a different voice (or instrument):

IMITATION: 'Danse Macabre' by Saint-Saëns

You can repeat a figure in longer notes:

RHYTHMIC AUGMENTATION: 'Danse Macabre' by Saint-Saëns

or shorter notes:

RHYTHMIC DIMINUTION: 'Variations and Fugue' by Britten

You can repeat a figure upside-down:

INVERSION (upside-down): 'Bye Bye Love' performed by Simon and Garfunkel

or backwards:

RETROGRADE (backwards): 'Variations and Fugue' by Britten

You can repeat a figure with *ornaments*:

ORNAMENTATION: 'Lucy Wan' performed by Martin Carthy

SOME MUSICAL TERMS EXPLAINED

Each of these terms appears in bold type in the main text where it is first mentioned.

ACCELERANDO (written as *accel.*) gradually faster.

ACCENT (looks like this: ➤) when you have an accent above or below a note or chord, you play this note or chord a little louder than the others.

ACCIDENTAL a sign which is written before some notes to show that they should be performed a semitone higher or lower. Examples of accidentals include the following:

G♮ (G natural) the same as G

G♯ (G sharp) a semitone higher than G

G♭ (G flat) a semitone lower than G

G✕ (G double sharp) a semitone higher than G♯

G♭♭ (G double flat) a semitone lower than G♭

ACCOMPANIMENT the part of the music which supports the main melody. For instance, in piano music, the right hand sometimes plays the melody, and the left hand plays the accompaniment.

AGOGO an African instrument, like two different-sized bells joined together, which is hit with a stick (there are no clappers in the bells). See the front cover of *Synchro Sound* by King Sunny Adé and his African Beats.

AIR really means the same as tune or melody. However, there are some quiet and melodious pieces of music called 'Air'; for example, the second movement of the Orchestral Suite No. 3 by Bach.

ALTO (also called 'contralto') low female voice. A male alto sings with a high, falsetto voice.

ARIA a song for solo voice usually with orchestral accompaniment. Most arias are part of operas or oratorios.

ARPEGGIO the notes of a chord performed one after another instead of simultaneously (see chapter 12).

ARRANGEMENT the writing of a previously composed piece of music for a specific instrument and/or vocal combination. Often this incorporates changes in elements such as rhythm, keys, dynamics, etc.

BARITONE a medium-pitched male voice. His high notes are not as high as those of a tenor, and his low notes are not as low as those of a bass.

BAROQUE 1. a period of music history, roughly 1600–1750
2. the style of music which was composed at this time.
Main features:
○ generally polyphonic texture, based on fugue. (However, Monteverdi and Purcell in particular wrote a lot of homophonic music.)
○ music is in clearly defined major and minor keys, and harmony is shown by 'figured bass'.
○ bass line is very important, often moving in steady quavers and implying the harmonies.
○ there is one mood (called 'affection') throughout each piece or movement.
○ melodies are constructed in long, flowing lines.
○ contrasts of many instruments (tutti) and few instruments (ripieno) are popular.
○ ornaments are used in melodies.
Major composers include Bach, Handel, Monteverdi, Purcell. Popular genres include opera, oratorio, fugue, suite, solo concerto, concerto grosso.

BASS 1. low male voice   2. lowest note in a chord, or lowest line in a piece of music   3. sometimes a bass guitar, string bass or bombardon is called 'bass'. (Bombardons are usually called 'B♭' or 'E♭' basses.)

BEAT 1. a rhythmic pulse which can be heard in much music   2. when conductors 'beat' time they move in time with the pulse of the music to show the speed of that pulse.

BLUES a style of music that was most popular between 1910 and 1940, and is still used in compositions today (see chapter 18). Main features:
○ sad lyrics – often about the feelings you experience when your loved one leaves you.
○ often in a major key, but with flattened 3rd and 7th. These are called 'blue' notes.
○ often there are 12 bars in each verse.
○ chords I(7), IV(7) and V(7) are frequently used in early blues, although later blues-style songs used many extra chords.

BOURRÉE a lively dance style, popular in Baroque times. The metre is in quadruple time, and the phrases begin on the last beat of the bar.

BRASS a family of instruments made from metal (not always brass), played by vibrating the lips into a mouthpiece.

BRASS BAND a combination of brass instruments, usually including cornets, flügelhorn, saxhorns, euphoniums, trombones and bombardons (B♭ and E♭ basses).

BREAK 1. a section in a rock or jazz composition where one instrument plays an accompanied solo passage   2. the place where the register of an instrument changes; e.g. B♭/B on a clarinet.

CADENCE see chapter 21 section 9.

CALL AND RESPONSE a form of song in which a leader sings a line (call) and a chorus sings a line (response) alternately. This is very common in sea shanties, work songs, field hollers, soul and gospel music.

CEILIDH a gathering with folk music and dancing.

CHORALE a solemn hymn tune, harmonised in four parts usually in simple quadruple or triple time, and almost invariably without any syncopation, e.g. 'O Sacred Head Ill-used' which is sung as part of the *St Matthew Passion* by Bach.

CHORD several notes played simultaneously (see chapter 12). Chordal means the same as *homophonic*.

CHORUS 1. a piece of music sung by a choir is sometimes called a chorus, especially choir movements of an opera or oratorio   2. part of a song that recurs, usually with the same lyrics each time.

CHROMATIC SCALE a scale made up of semitones. A chromatic passage is one which involves part of the chromatic scale.

CLASSICAL 1. all the music composed in the styles of Western art music, including Renaissance, Baroque, Classical, Romantic, etc.   2. art music; for instance, Indian art music is often called 'classical'   3. The musical style that was popular between about 1750 and 1810. Main features:
○ a concern for elegance and grace.
○ melodies constructed largely from four- or eight-bar phrases, with a clear pull towards the keynote (tonic).
○ clear, homophonic texture (although Mozart in particular used counterpoint).
○ changes of mood and dynamics during a piece or movement. Major composers include Mozart and Haydn. Popular genres include sonata, symphony, solo concerto, opera, string quartet.

CLEF a sign at the beginning of a stave of music which shows where each pitch comes on that stave (see chapter 21 section 2).

CODA a finishing section of a piece of music or a movement (see *Sonata form*)

COMPOUND TIME a metre in which each main beat has three faster beats to it; for example: $\frac{6}{8}$, $\frac{9}{8}$, $\frac{12}{8}$ . . . (see chapter 21 section 3).

CONCERTO a composition for a solo instrument with orchestra, usually with three movements, e.g. Piano Concerto in C, K467 by Mozart.

CONCORD a harmonious chord. Major chords, minor chords, and the intervals of a 3rd, perfect 5th, 6th and octave are concords. Other chords and intervals can also be concords, depending on the context of the rest of the music.

COR ANGLAIS (also called 'English horn') a woodwind instrument similar to but lower than an oboe.

COUNTER-MELODY a melody that you hear at the same time as the main melody.

COUNTER-TENOR a male voice higher than a tenor, with a range roughly equivalent to that of an alto.

CRESCENDO see *Dynamics*.

DIMINUENDO see *Dynamics*.

DIMINUTION where a melody is changed by having all its note values made shorter.

DISCORD a chord which does not sound harmonious, i.e. any chord which is not a concord.

DOUBLE STOPPING a technique of string-playing by which two notes are played simultaneously.

DRONE one or more notes played all the way through a piece, or a section of a piece, of music.

DUET a piece of music for two voices or instruments.

DUPLE TIME see *Metre*.

DYNAMICS the loudness or softness of sounds. This is shown by the following symbols:

pp (pianissimo) = very quiet
p (piano) = quiet
mp (mezzo piano) = fairly quiet
mf (mezzo forte) = fairly loud
f (forte) = loud
ff (fortissimo) = very loud
 (crescendo) = getting louder (also written *cresc.*)
 (diminuendo) = getting quieter (also written *dim.*)

ELECTRONIC MUSIC 1. music which is produced by electronic means, e.g. by a synthesiser   2. music which is produced by electronic or non-electronic means, recorded on tape, and altered by manipulating the tape, e.g. *Poème Electronique* by Varèse.

ELEMENTS OF MUSIC the ingredients of music: melody, rhythm, texture, tone colour, form, dynamics.

ENGLISH HORN see *Cor anglais*

EPISODE a section of music which is different from and occurs between the main themes.

EXPOSITION see *Sonata form*.

FEEDBACK a high-pitched sound produced by electronic speakers, occasionally used in rock music.

FIFTH the interval between one note and another, five notes higher up in the scale, e.g. C-G, D-A, E-B (see chapter 21 section 5).

FIGURE (also called 'motif') a few notes played one after another. Melodic figures involve different pitches, but rhythmic figures do not (see chapter 1).

FORM the way in which different sections of music are put together. Some examples are ternary form (chapter 5), variations (chapter 10) and rondo (chapter 19).

FOURTH the interval between one note and another, four notes higher up in the scale, e.g. C-F, D-G, E-A (see chapter 21 section 5).

FUGUE a musical form based on imitation, with a polyphonic texture. There are main melodies (called subjects), and counter-melodies (called counter-subjects) and these are repeated in higher and lower registers, and different keys, sometimes in augmentation or diminution; e.g. the fugue from 'Variations and Fugue on a Theme of Purcell' by Britten.

GAVOTTE a lively dance in quadruple time. The phrases begin on the third beat of the bar, e.g. the third movement of the Orchestral Suite No. 3 by Bach.

GRAPHIC SCORE a copy of music which contains various artistic shapes. These communicate to the performers roughly how the music should be performed (see chapter 16).

HARMONY when you have more than one note at a time. To harmonise a melody, play or sing other notes at the same time as that melody.

HOMOPHONY (sometimes called 'chordal') a musical texture which consists of a melody accompanied by harmonies, e.g. 'Love Me Tender' by Elvis Presley.

IMITATION when a melodic figure is repeated by a different voice or instrument.

INTERLUDE 1. a section of a composition which does not involve any of the main themes   2. a piece of music played between the scenes of a play or opera, e.g. the 'Sea Interludes' from *Peter Grimes* by Britten.

INTERVAL the distance between two notes (see chapter 21 section 5).

INTRODUCTION a section which begins a piece of music but does not contain the first main theme.

INVERSION a musical figure performed upside-down.

JIG (also called 'gigue') a lively dance in compound time.

KEY involves the scale on which a piece of music is based. For example, a piece in the key of G major has G as its tonal centre (keynote), and uses mainly the notes of a G major scale. See chapter 21 sections 6 and 7.

LEGATO smoothly.

LINE the part performed by one voice or instrument. The highest notes in a musical texture are sometimes called the soprano line, the next highest the alto line, the third highest the tenor line, and the lowest the bass, even when all the lines are played by the same instrument, e.g. the piano.

MAJOR 1. a type of scale (see chapter 21 section 6); music which is based on this scale is said to be in a major key 2. a type of interval (see chapter 21 section 6) 3. a type of chord, consisting of a root, a major 3rd and a perfect 5th (see chapter 21 section 8).

MASS the main form of worship in the Roman Catholic religion – the celebration of the Eucharist. The sections which are usually set to music are called 'Kyrie' (Lord Have Mercy), 'Gloria' (Glory to God), 'Sanctus' (Holy, Holy, Holy), 'Benedictus' (Blessed Be He) and 'Agnus Dei' (Lamb of God).

MELODY (also called a 'tune') a line of notes varying in pitch and rhythm.

METRE the way that beats are grouped (see chapter 21 section 3). Often the beats are grouped in a metre of two (also called duple time), three (triple time) or four (quadruple time). For example:

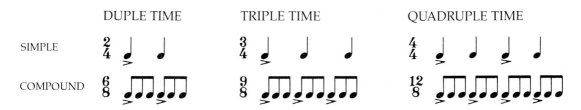

> = Stronger beat

MEZZO SOPRANO a female voice of medium pitch.

MINOR 1. a type of scale (see chapter 21 section 6); music which is based on this scale is said to be in a minor key 2. a type of interval (see chapter 21 section 6); 3. a type of chord, consisting of a root, a minor 3rd and a perfect 5th (see chapter 21 section 8).

MINUET a stately dance in moderate triple time, e.g the third movement of the Clarinet Trio by Mozart.

MODE an arrangement of tones and semitones to make a scale. The most common modes are the major and minor scales.

MONOPHONY a musical texture consisting of a melody on its own, e.g. *Syrinx* by Debussy.

MOVEMENT a self-contained main section of a large composition such as a symphony or concerto.

MUSIQUE CONCRÈTE music made from recorded sounds. Both sounds from nature and manmade sounds can be used, and the tape on which they are recorded is sometimes manipulated to change the quality of the sounds.

NATIONALIST a type of Romantic music concerned with creating specifically national styles as distinct from the dominant Austrian and German styles created by Beethoven, Schubert and others. Major composers include Smetana, Dvořák, Greig and Glinka.

OCTAVE the interval between one note and another, eight notes higher up in the scale, e.g. C-C', D-D', E-E' (see chapter 21 section 6).

OPEN STRING on stringed instruments, strings are 'open' when they are played without having a finger pressed on them. The open strings of the more common stringed instruments are tuned like this:

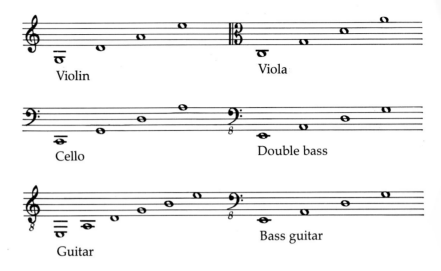

Violin   Viola

Cello   Double bass

Guitar   Bass guitar

OPERA a play that is set to music for solo singers and (usually) chorus, with orchestral accompaniment. In Baroque and Classical times, the soloists' music would consist mainly of recitative and arias, but since the time of Wagner these distinctions have become blurred, e.g. *Peter Grimes* by Britten.

ORATORIO similar to opera, but different in two important ways: a. it is performed as a concert without costumes or acting, and b. the words have a religious meaning, e.g. the *Messiah* by Handel.

ORNAMENT a decoration of one note in a melody. Common ornaments include the following:

Trill (also called 'shake')

written   played

Trills may be played differently, depending on the style and tempo of the music.

Appoggiatura

written   played

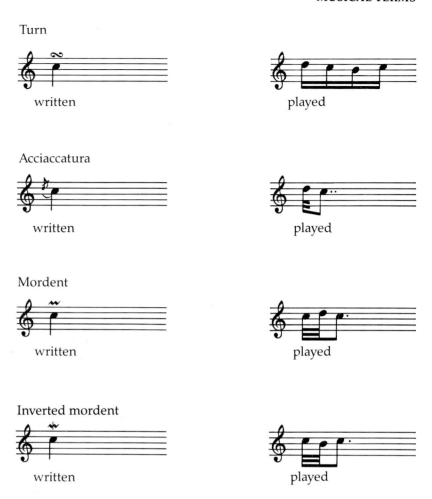

Turn — written / played

Acciaccatura — written / played

Mordent — written / played

Inverted mordent — written / played

OSTINATO a musical figure which is repeated many times (see chapter 6).

OVERTURE a piece of instrumental music in one movement. In Baroque and Classical times, overtures were usually written as introductions to operas, oratorios and plays. In Romantic times it became common to compose overtures which were unconnected with any of these forms, e.g. Concert Overture *1812* by Tchaikovsky.

PASSING NOTE in harmony, a passing note is one which does not fit with the chord it is sounded with, but moves by step between two notes that do.

PASSION an oratorio in which the words are about the suffering and death of Jesus, e.g. 'The Passion According to St Matthew' (also called the *St Matthew Passion*) by Bach.

PAVANE a slow dance in quadruple time which was popular in the sixteenth and seventeenth centuries.

PERCUSSION a type of instrument that is made to sound by being hit, shaken or scraped. See chapters 10 and 16.

PERDENDOSI dying away.

PHRASE a musical phrase is similar to a phrase in language. When you speak, you group your words in a way that will make sense. When you perform music, you group your notes in a way that will make musical sense. Each of these groups of notes is called a phrase, and is shown by this sign: ⌒

PITCH relative high-/low-ness of sounds.

PIZZICATO (written as *pizz.*) an effect you can get with orchestral string instruments by plucking the strings instead of using a bow.

POLYPHONY (also called 'counterpoint' and 'contrapuntal') 1. a musical texture in which you hear two or more melodies at the same time 2. synthesisers or keyboards which can play two or more notes simultaneously are sometimes described as polyphonic.

POLYRHYTHM a musical texture in which you hear two or more rhythms simultaneously.

PONTICELLO (written as *pont.*) an unusual effect you can get with orchestral string instruments by drawing the bow across the string very close to the bridge.

PRELUDE really a piece of music which comes before something else, e.g. a Prelude and Fugue. However, some composers have written preludes which are unconnected with other events; e.g. 'The Girl with the Flaxen Hair' from Debussy's first book of *Préludes*.

PROGRAMME 1. a booklet describing a concert, opera, etc. 2. a story, poem or idea associated with a particular piece of music (see chapter 17).

QUADRUPLE TIME see *Metre*.

QUARTET music for four voices (often soprano, alto, tenor and bass) or instruments. String quartets are written for two violins, viola and cello.

RAGA a type of melody based on a scale pattern, and used as a basis for improvisation in the classical music of north India. Ragas are associated with moods such as peacefulness or loneliness, and also with a particular time of day.

RANGE the total notes (lowest to highest) that a particular voice or instrument can produce.

RALLENTANDO (written as *rall.*) getting slower.

RECITATIVE a type of solo singing used mainly in operas and oratorios. Recitatives are useful for dialogue and for telling the story, because they let the words be sung quickly and clearly, but they are usually not as melodic or expressive as arias.

REEL a quick and smoothly-flowing dance in simple quadruple time.

REGGAE a musical style from Jamaica (see chapter 14). Main features:

○ dress style associated with Rastafarians, including hair in long, tight plaits (dreadlocks) and woollen hats in green, gold and red.

○ lyrics usually sung in a Jamaican dialect, and often associated with Rastafarian beliefs.

○ loud bass riffs played on bass guitar.

○ harmonies often limited to a few chords, which are repeated many times in the same sequence.

○ slow quadruple time with accents on the second and fourth beat of every bar.

Reggae stars include Bob Marley and the Wailers, Peter Tosh and UB40.

REGISTER the high- or low-ness of sounds; for example, if a group of notes is high-pitched the notes are described as being in a high register.

RENAISSANCE 1. a period of music (and art) history, roughly 1400–1600 2. the style of music which was composed at that time. Main features:

○ music not in major or minor scales but in several different modes, so that the tonal centre is not so obvious as in later music.

○ much (but not all) of the surviving Renaissance music is church music often for unaccompanied choir.

○ vocal music is generally polyphonic, and usually based on short phrases which are developed using a lot of imitation.

○ flowing melodies and harmonies. Leaps in the melodies are usually followed by steps. Discords in the harmonies are usually followed by concords.

Major composers include Josquin, Palestrina, Byrd and Giovanni Gabrieli. Popular genres include motet, anthem, mass, madrigal, variations on a ground.

REQUIEM Roman Catholic Mass for the Dead.

REST a musical silence. See chapter 21 section 1.

RETROGRADE a musical phrase or subject played backwards is sometimes described as 'retrograde'.

RHYTHM the way music moves through time. Composers organise short sounds and long sounds, with or without beat and metre, choosing fast or slow tempos. all of which go to make the rhythm of the music.

RIFF a melodic figure, usually in the bass, repeated many times. Common in many types of popular music and jazz.

RITARDANDO (written as *ritard.* or *rit.*) hold back; i.e. get slower.

ROCK several styles of music are called 'Rock', including Rock'n'Roll (e.g. Chuck Berry), Progressive Rock (e.g. Led Zeppelin) and Punk Rock (e.g. The Sex Pistols). In addition, much disco music is sometimes called Rock.

ROCK STEADY (also called 'blue beat') a type of reggae, popular in the 1960s, usually a little faster than modern reggae. Rock steady stars include Toots and the Maytals.

ROMANTIC 1. A period of music (and art and literature) history, roughly 1810–1900 2. The style of music which was composed at that time. Main features:
○ very obviously emotional music, with dramatic contrasts of dynamics, registers, tone colours and tempos.
○ song-like melodies, often above a homophonic texture.
○ classical forms expanded, leading to some very large-scale compositions.
○ music for soloists designed to show off the brilliance of their technique (instrumental technique improved enormously).
Major composers include Beethoven, Brahms, Wagner and Chopin. Popular genres include song, symphony, opera, overture, solo concerto, sonata, symphonic poem, requiem.

RONDO a musical form (see chapter 19). Sonata rondo is a form which combines rondo form with sonata form. Many of Mozart's and Beethoven's 'rondos' are really in sonata rondo form.

SCALE a selection of notes arranged from lowest to highest (or highest to lowest). Many pieces of music are based on a scale (see chapter 21 section 6).

SCORE a copy which contains all the musical parts of a composition in written form.

SECOND the interval between one note and another, two notes higher up in the scale, e.g. C-D, D-E, E-F (see chapter 21 section 5).

SEMITONE the smallest interval in most Western music, e.g. C-C♯, D-D♯, E-F. Another name for a semitone is a minor second (see chapter 21 section 5).

SEQUENCE when a melodic figure or phrase is repeated at higher or lower pitch; e.g. bars 3–6 of 'Variations and Fugue on a Theme of Purcell' by Britten (chapter 11).

SEVENTH the interval between one note and another, seven notes higher up in the scale, e.g. C-B, D-C, E-D (see chapter 21 section 5).

SFORZANDO (usually written *sf* or *sfz*) a strong accent.

SHEKERE an African instrument like a large maraca, but with beads on the outside. See the front cover of *Synchro Sound* by King Sunny Adé and his African Beats.

SIMPLE TIME a metre in which each main beat has two faster beats to it (see chapter 21 section 3).

SIXTH the interval between one note and another, six notes higher up in the scale, e.g. C-A, D-B, E-C (see chapter 21 section 5).

SOLO a piece of music for one performer, with or without accompaniment.

SONATA a composition for a solo instrument with piano, or simply a solo piano (e.g. The 'Moonlight' Sonata by Beethoven). Usually sonatas are fairly long compositions, often with several movements.

SONATA FORM a musical form popular throughout the Classical and Romantic periods. At its most simple, it consists of two themes or groups of themes in different keys, linked by a bridge passage. These are presented in the first section (called 'exposition'), varied, and played in different keys in the middle section (called 'development' section), and played with some alterations in the final section (called 'recapitulation'). There is usually a 'coda' to finish off the movement, and sometimes an 'introduction' to begin it.

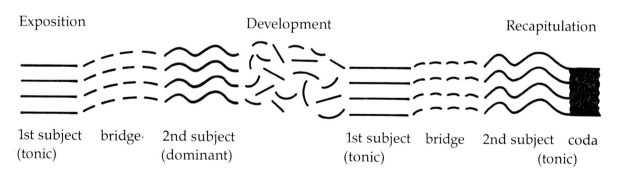

Exposition			Development	Recapitulation		
1st subject (tonic)	bridge	2nd subject (dominant)		1st subject (tonic)	bridge	2nd subject / coda (tonic)

The first movement of *Eine Kleine Nachtmusik* by Mozart is a clear and simple example of sonata form.

SONG CYCLE a group of songs which are meant to be performed together, usually because the words are all about the same topic.

SOPRANO a high female voice.

SPACING the way the notes of a chord are organised into high, medium and low pitches.

STACCATO the symbol for staccato is a dot (·) above or below a note or chord. Staccato notes or chords are played shorter than written.

STEEL BAND a combination of instruments, popular in the Caribbean, called 'pans'. These are made from large or small oil drums, with their heads beaten into shapes so that they make sounds of different pitches when hit.

STRETTO a device used in fugues. A subject is played and, before it is finished, another voice starts on the same subject. The effect can be an increase of tension or excitement in the music.

STRINGS types of instrument on which wire or gut strings are stretched over a resonating box and made to sound by their being hit (harpsichord), bowed (violin) or plucked (guitar).

STYLE the overall effect of a musical composition (or work of art). This is produced by the way the composer organises all the musical elements in the composition.

SUBJECT a melody or theme (see *Fugue* and *Sonata form*).

SUITE a piece of instrumental music in several movements. A Baroque suite consisted of movements in dance styles; e.g. Orchestral Suite No. 3 by Bach.

SYMPHONY a large orchestral composition, usually in four contrasting movements (see chapters 3, 11 and 12).

TABLA Indian drums (see chapter 4).

TEMPO speed. Common indications of tempo:
grave (very slow)
largo (slow and stately)/lento (slow)
adagio (slow)
moderato (moderate speed)
andante (leisurely)
allegro (fast)
presto (very fast)
These are sometimes coupled with the words 'meno' (less) or 'molto' (very). A common way of showing extremes is to put '-issimo' on the end of a word, e.g. prestissimo (extremely fast). Also see *Accelerando, Rallentando, Ritardando*.

TENOR a high male voice.

TEXTURE the effect of melodies and harmonies together; i.e. thick (many sounds simultaneously) or thin (a few sounds simultaneously). See also *Homophony, Monophony, Polyphony.*

THEME an important melody which occurs more than once in a piece of music. Occasionally a theme may be just a melodic figure, or a rhythmic figure; e.g. in 'Ionisation' by Varèse.

THIRD the interval between one note and another, three notes higher up in the scale, e.g. C-E, D-F, E-G (see chapter 21 section 5).

TIMBRE see *Tone colour.*

TIME see *Metre.*

TIME SIGNATURE a sign which usually comes at the beginning of a piece of music, and shows how many beats there are in each bar, and the value of the beat (see chapter 21 section 3).

TONALITY the type of scale on which a composition, or part of a composition is based. The most common tonalities in Western music are major and minor tonalities. Music without any tonal centre is called 'atonal'.

TONE 1. the quality of a sound, e.g. a thin, or a reedy or a full tone 2. a major second (see chapter 21 section 5).

TONE COLOUR (also called 'timbre') a particular quality of sound. The difference between a flute playing a note and a clarinet playing the same note at the same pitch and volume is a difference in tone colour.

TONIC the keynote. See chapter 21 section 6.

TRANSPOSE change the pitch. For example, a piece in C major can be transposed into D major by raising the pitch of each note by a tone. Some instruments generally have their music written out already transposed, to make it easier to play.

TREMOLANDO (written as *tremolo* or *trem.*) 1. a rapid repetition of a single note 2. a rapid playing of two notes alternately.

written   played

TRIAD a chord made of two intervals of a third ; e.g. a C major triad is made of C, E and G.

TRILL see *Ornament*.

TRIO 1. a group of three performers   2. the music written for three performers. Common trios include piano trio (piano, violin and cello) and string trio (violin, viola and cello)   3. the middle section of a minuet and trio.

TRIPLE TIME see *Metre*.

TUNED PERCUSSION percussion instruments that can play notes of definite pitch; e.g. xylophone.

UNISON one melodic line performed by all voices and/or instruments, producing a monophonic texture.

UNTUNED PERCUSSION percussion instruments that play no definite pitches, e.g. tambourine.

VALVE a device on some brass instruments for making small changes of pitch. If valve instruments are played without their valves being pressed down, they can play only a limited number of notes.

VARIATION sometimes music is repeated with various important changes. This changed repeat is called a variation.

WHOLE TONE SCALE a scale made up entirely of intervals of a tone. See chapter 8, chapter 21 section 6.

WOODWIND a type of instrument (not necessarily made of wood) which is made to sound by being blown, either directly (e.g. recorder) or by vibrating a reed (e.g. clarinet).